CONCILIUM

Religion in the Eighties

CONCILIUM

Concilium 190 (2/1987): Liturgy

CONCILIUM

List of Members

Advisory Committee: Liturgy

Directors:

Mary Collins OSB	Wake Forest, NC	USA
David Power	Washington, DC	USA

Members:

Ad Blijlevens CSsR	Voerendaal	The Netherlands
Boris Bobrinskoy	Boulogne	France
Londi Boka di Mpasi SJ	Kinshasa-Gombe	Zaire
Anscar Chupungco OSB	Rome	Italy
Geoffrey Cuming	Oxford	England
Irénée-Henri Dalmais OP	Paris	France
Luigi Della Torre	Rome	Italy
Michel Dujarier	Allada	Bénin
Joseph Gelineau SJ	Moret sur Loing	France
Maucyr Gibin	Sao Paulo, SP	Brazil
Kathleen Hughes RSCJ	Chicago, Ill.	USA
Denis Hurley OMI	Durban	South Africa
Aidan Kavanagh OSB	New Haven, Conn.	USA
Guy Lapointe	Montreal	Canada
Juan Llopis	Barcelona	Spain
Gerard Lukken	Tilburg	The Netherlands
Luis Maldonado	Madrid	Spain
Paul Puthanangady SDB	Bangalore	India
Gail Ramshaw-Schmidt	Bronx, NY	USA
Heinrich Rennings	Paderborn	West Germany
Philippe Rouillard OSB	Rome	Italy
Anton Scheer	Rosmalen	The Netherlands
Kevin Seasoltz OSB	Washington, DC	USA
Robert Taft SJ	Notre Dame, Ind.	USA
Evangelista Vilanova OSB	Montserrat	Spain
Geoffrey Wainwright	Durham, NC	USA
Herman Wegman	Driebergen-Rijsenburg	The Netherlands

THE FATE OF CONFESSION

Edited by
Mary Collins
and
David Power

English Language Editor
Marcus Lefébure

T. & T. CLARK LTD
Edinburgh

April 1987
T. & T. Clark Ltd, 59 George Street, Edinburgh EH2 2LQ
ISBN: 0 567 30070 6

ISSN: 0010-5236

Typeset by C. R. Barber & Partners (Highlands) Ltd, Fort William
Printed by Page Brothers (Norwich) Ltd

Concilium: Published February, April, June, August, October, December.
Subscriptions 1987: UK: £24.95 (including postage and packing); USA: US$45.00
(including air mail postage and packing); Canada: Canadian$55.00 (including air mail
postage and packing); other countries: £24.95 (including postage and packing).

95835

CONTENTS

Part III
Ecclesial and Theological Traditions

CONCILIUM 190 Special Column

Norbert Greinacher

On the Way to an Ecumenical Assembly for Peace

DIETRICH BONHOEFFER, in a speech on 28 August 1934 at a joint session of the World Alliance for Promoting International Friendship through the Churches and of the Ecumenical Council for Practical Christendom held in Fanö, Denmark, said the following:

> *Only the one great Ecumenical Council of the Holy Church of Christ over all the world can speak out so that the world, though it gnashes its teeth, will have to hear, so that the people will rejoice because the Church of Christ in the name of Christ has taken the weapons from the hands of their sons, forbidden war and proclaimed the peace of Christ against the raging world. (*No Rusty Swords, *p. 291)*

This prophetic word was not heeded at the time. But around fifty years later, in 1983, the international conference of the World Council of Churches meeting in Vancouver, Canada, took up a proposal of the Evangelical Church in East Germany and decided to hold a world conference of the churches for justice, peace and the maintenance of creation.

This resolution was not without effect. In June 1985 the Evangelical Church concluded its Assembly Day in Düsseldorf by issuing the following appeal:

> *We beg the churches of the world to call a council of peace. Peace is today the condition of the survival of the human race. It is not guaranteed. The Christian churches must call an ecumenical council*

for the sake of peace and assume joint responsibility for uttering a word that humankind cannot ignore. Time presses. We call upon the leaders of the churches to do everything in their power to ensure a meeting of the council as soon as possible. We call upon church communities to give the summons to this council their express support.

The central committee of the World Council of Churches vigorously endorsed this appeal at its meeting in August 1985 and called for national and international initiatives in this sense. The executive committee of the World Council pursued the matter when it met between 9 and 15 March 1986 in Kinshasha, Zaire, and formulated substantive and organisational decisions. Pope John-Paul II invited the great world religions to take part in a day of prayer on 27 October 1986, which left a great impression on public opinion throughout the world.

In November 1986 a consultation was held in Glion, Switzerland, to prepare for an ecumenical assembly, and five official representatives of the Catholic Church, from the Justice and Peace commission and the Secretariat for Christian Unity, took part. The central committee of the World Council at its meeting in Geneva in January 1987 invited Christian churches of the world to take part in this ecumenical assembly of Christians in the year 1990:

The churches are summoned to 'put down the mighty' and to declare themselves in every situation on the side of life.

A 'northern conference' of the churches from the countries party to the Helsinki Accords for Security and Cooperation in Europe is to be held in 1988 in order to prepare for the ecumenical assembly

In the space that remains a few important points concerning the concept as well as the urgency of this plan for an ecumenical assembly for peace need to be made.

We should not allow ourselves to be bogged down by useless squabbles about the name of this assembly. One can only heartily endorse what Carl Friedrich von Weizsäcker said in June 1986 in the Evangelical Academy of Tutzing in West Germany:

The assembly will not be convoked under the name 'Council' and should not be convoked under the name 'Conference'. 'World Assembly' of Christians for Justice, Peace and the Maintenance of Creation is one possible name. If the assembly turns out to speak as it should, people may then say: This was a council.

Of critical importance is the active participation of churches and Christians of the Third World. *It must be clearly understood that, while the inhabitants of the northern hemisphere live under the threat, above all, of the atomic holocaust and many of those who inhabit the southern hemisphere go hungry and even starve, the North-South conflict is bound up with the East-West conflict and that what Christians must do is precisely to be in solidarity with the needs of others.*

As the third great danger hanging over the existence of the human race the ecological crisis *that challenges both halves of the earth indifferently must be taken into account. The plenary session of the World Council in Vancouver was therefore well advised to include the maintenance of creation as the third theme.*

The participation of the Catholic Church, *and as an active co-responsible and inviting party alongside the churches represented in the World Council, poses a grave problem. At the moment the outlook for such a sharing in responsibility and cooperation on the part of the Catholic Church is good.*

What will be quite decisive for the success of this ecumemical assembly is what has been called the 'conciliar process': *it is not a question of a meeting of Church officials and delegates coming to some theoretical resolution but of this meeting being prepared from below and its contents being actively discussed. Not a single church community should be excluded from this conciliar process.*

It will be no easy task at the end of this conciliar process to come to conclusions that embody both *the radicality of the* prophetic traditions *of the Old and the New Testaments regarding justice, peace and the maintenance of creation* and *the* reality *and political possibilities of our time.*

A great deal is at stake. The credibility of the Christian message and of the Christian churches *depends on whether they can give an authentic Christian answer to the three issues that hang over human existence.*

May Christian women and men this time—and not as in 1934— understand the 'signs of the times' and open themselves up to the working of the Spirit.

Translated by John London

THE FATE OF CONFESSION

Editorial

FOUR YEARS after the 1983 Synod of Bishops convened to discuss 'Reconciliation and Penance in the Mission of the Church', good pastoral and theological reasons exist to inquire about the *fate of confession*. The designated synod topic and much of the preparatory work of the national episcopal conferences promised a stimulating exchange on a matter vital to the Roman Catholic Church's identity. After all, in the Church's first generation Paul had summed up the significance of Christian discipleship by saying to the Corinthians that he and they were *ambassadors of reconciliation* and that to them had been entrusted God's message to the world: Be reconciled! (2 Cor. 5:19–21). It was not unreasonable to expect a lively discussion on the Roman Catholic Church's role in the ministry of reconciliation of the nations, in the reconciliation of the human race with the planet earth and the whole universe, in the reconciliation of the churches, in the reconciliation of cultures, in the work of reconciliation within families and households and between the sexes, in short, in every aspect of gathering and integrating whatever in human life is broken and scattered.

Somehow, between the 1982 inception and the 1984 dénoument of the synod, an unnecessary and untimely *constriction of vision occurred*. Individual confession of sin became too central an issue for the synod and at the same time confession was explored too superficially to yield any measurable pastoral or theological gains. In the end, conventional approaches to sacramental confession and absolution were reaffirmed, but the reaffirmations seemed not to make much of current pastoral experience nor to consider contemporary theological reflection on the tradition of individual confession in the light of cultural realities. Old verities and familiar ecclesiastical disciplines were underscored, but the hard questions of our day were not faced up to. Yet the fate of sacramental confession is tied finally not to abstract principle but to human beings in history.

The editors of this *Concilium* issue might have looked at particular sacramental rites of reconciliation, the act of confession within the ritual structure, and the appropriate performance of such liturgical rites in the light of the Synod's work. We took another tack in preparing this issue, choosing rather to probe many facets of the Christian tradition in order to understand the *human dynamics as well as the religious significance of any liturgical confession of sin.*

A first set of essays establishes the contemporary problematic for the discussion. *Gail Ramshaw-Schmidt*, in what is perhaps the most provocative essay for assessing the long-term future of confession, invites readers to acknowledge that sin is one, but only one, of a cluster of quite traditional ways of naming the human experience of *limit*. Other scriptural ways of evoking limit—death, injustice, disease, chaos—elicit other images for attending to our condition: rebirth, justice, wholeness, meaning. The correlatives sin and forgiveness of sin exhaust neither our experiences nor the biblical witness to our human condition and our human need. What are we to make of these other liturgically underdeveloped insights into being human? Might they give rise to other rituals of reconciliation?

Catherine Dooley presents an overview of the proceedings of the 1983 synod from its preparatory phases to the closing Apostolic Exhortation, noting by reference to synod documents how the body's focus narrowed from its convening to its conclusion. Because the synod reaffirmed the teaching of the Council of Trent as normative for the Church's sacramental ministry of reconciliation, the editors asked *Dionisio Borobio* to look again at that pivotal moment in the Church's life. The bishops at Trent had quite specific things to say about confession of sin. In what sense(s), if any, did they have the final word?

A second group of essays addresses pastoral realities. Confession of sin is a means, not an end in itself. *Konrad Baumgartner* investigates the desired end, namely, continuing Christian conversion. In his investigation, he looks also at the various ways in which the Christian people mediate conversion for one another, situating the believer's act of confession of personal sin to an ordained minister within the larger conversion process. The editors asked *Michael Sievernich* to explore the phenomenon of *social sin*, at once as pervasive as the air we breathe and evidently just as elusive to our perception. If the synod failed to establish the link between the phenomenon of social sin and the tradition of individual confession, nevertheless, late twentieth century religious sensibilities and ecclesial developments suggest that the Church is at a new moment in its self-understanding. The *missing link between traditional private confession and social sin* is decisive for the future of confession, perhaps even for the future of the church.

Children's confessions as we know them are a twentieth century invention, a very late development of ecclesiastical discipline. *Norbert Mette* reports on the origins of the discipline and reflects critically on some of the assumptions and implications of early childhood confession of sin. *Kabasele Lumbala* sets out for *Concilium* readers some contemporary *Black African efforts* to come to terms with its own experiences of sin, confession, and reconciliation. Because it is easy to forget that the Roman Catholic tradition of confessing sin has a history and that its present discipline has emerged from a series of meetings between the Gospel and cultures, giving some attention to emerging practices within the young churches can have the secondary benefit of shedding light on what has already taken shape in Roman Catholicism.

A third collection of articles explores the witness of the *broader ecclesial and theological traditions*. These provide another route toward understanding and contextualising Roman Catholic approaches to confession of sin. Three are retrospective. *Cesare Giraudo* looks at the matter of sin and its confession as a partial expression of *covenant faith* in Israel, as one moment in the larger covenant confession of God's goodness and of Israel's own trust and hope. *Frans van de Paverd* reviews the range of traditional teachings which are the foundation for the *Eastern churches'* dealings with sin and reconciliation. *Frank Senn* presents and interprets the discipline of the Western churches which emerged from the sixteenth century *Protestant reformation*. Finally, *Geoffrey Wainwright* looks forward to a future event, the act of confession of sin as a necessary step in any historical process for the reconciliation of the churches themselves. Drawing upon the wisdom of the whole tradition, he proposes possible procedures and offers his reflection on the theological and pastoral significance of such an event.

David Power's editorial conclusion suggests additional ways to understand, appreciate, exploit, and even develop the wisdom of religious confession within the church of Jesus Christ. What this *Concilium* discussion on the fate of confession has most in common with the 1983 synod documents is its character as one part of a *continuing conversation* within the Church on human involvement in the mystery of conversion.

MARY COLLINS, OSB

PART 1

Contemporary Problematic

Gail Ramshaw-Schmidt

Sin: One Image of Human Limitation

IT IS not surprising that the twentieth century Church finds itself confused concerning its use of the category 'sins'. Of course there has never been absolute consensus concerning this complex idea. What is sin to one person has not necessarily been sin to another. For example, the tradition of Christian pacificism illustrates a historic disagreement over the morality of national defence: we do not agree whether defensive warfare is sin. But contemporary confusion runs deeper than debates over whether specific acts are sins. Religion sees God answering the needs occasioned by human limits: because we are creatures, we need a god. In the West the dominant image for our creatureliness, the recurring model of human limitation, has been sin. *But sin has not been the sole image for human need*, and presently it is not the existentially operative image for many Christians. The intellectual question parallels the Church's dilemma over confession. Do people, ought people, attend confession? Why, why not? But before we can address the pastoral implications of this issue, we must step back to examine the image sin and to consider *alternative images for human limitation.*

1. SELF-AWARENESS, SIN AND SINS

The task of Western consciousness has been *self-awareness before God*. The plays of the Greeks, the writings of the philosophers, the poems of the prophets, the religious and cultural rituals of past civilisations, all attest to the same struggle: given the existence of God, we must come to know ourselves. Granting belief in a personal deity, the Westerner comes to self-knowledge. Even Don Quixote conceived of his mission as a service to God as he cried out

3

in highest comic irony, 'I know who I am!' Contemporary atheistic philosophy as well stands in the tradition of those whose language was developed within religious presuppositions. The repeated Western answer to this quest has been that we come to know ourselves as limited before God who is limitless. That we are not God is the first level of philosophical inquiry, and *the most common image used to label this limitation is sin*. Linguistic sophistication teaches us how to trace the development of this our dominant model: Paul Ricoeur's *Symbolism of Evil* suggests one key to understanding the Judaeo-Christian identification of evil with sin. The origin of the word sin in the literal verb 'to miss the mark' reminds us of the metaphorical nature of this label for human limitation.

The literature of the ancient Western world suggests that the *earliest understanding of sin is actually closer to our word sins*. That is, human beings committed specific immoral acts for which the deity holds them responsible, or they perpetuated specific antisocial actions which rendered them unclean before God and the community. Oedipus is searching to know who he is, and in true Western fashion his discovery is not only who are his parents, but also that before God he is the guilty one. The people of Israel after the Exodus define themselves as those set free, and in this process of self-knowledge they receive the tables of the law. Theological reflection evolves the primitive list of specific infractions into the philosophical concept of sin. Sin becomes the dominant Western language used to describe the reality of being human. Sin is the demonstrable separation of the human from the divine, a label for the distance between a limitless God and limited humankind.

In order to analyse the image sin, let us quickly trace its *preeminence as a Christian category for human limitation*. The God of the Hebrews is described throughout the Old Testament as a God of judgment and mercy. This implies a people who sin and need forgiveness. One aspect of the Garden of Eden story is that Eve and Adam are guilty of sin. The prophetic literature calls the people to self-consciousness over sins—specific examples of idolatry, selfishness, and injustice—and over sin—the terrifying distance from a saving God. The gospels interweave narratives of the life of Jesus with the interpretation that what Jesus did was to forgive sin. In Mark 2 the miracle of the healing of the paralytic is made a sign of the essential task of God's forgiving sins. The tradition of Western theology has been shaped to great degree by what we might call 'male mid-life crisis theologians': Paul, Augustine, Luther. Like Dante in the first stanza of *The Inferno*, these men were wandering in mid-life and discovered that their search for God and for peace in truth was impeded by the human limitation they identified as sin. Anselm's theory of atonement which exercised enormous influence over theology and liturgical practice also conceived of the great human problem, distance from God, as being occasioned by sin and of the Church as the agent of a forgiving judge, meting out forgiveness for sins. Still today acts of confession are a pastoral application of this image. The faithful are guilty of sin which must be forgiven before the joy of divine life can be celebrated.

2. CONFESSING IN THE FACE OF MORAL CONFUSION

Do we confess *sin or sins*? The confusion between these two words is no small matter. 'To confess sin' is to acknowledge one's distance from God, to declare oneself human before God. To confess sin, like to confess the creed, is to state self-awareness. But 'to confess sins' has come to mean a grovelling under guilt, a listing of infractions, a laundry list of what must be cleansed before one can come to the table. Theologians hope to teach that the greatest human limitation is sin, that sin is the fact of distance from God, and that God bridges this distance with mercy. Yet catechesis continues to define sin as observed in sinful acts. Not the great prophets of Israel nor contemporary preaching has succeeded in describing sin other than by evoking lists of sins. In the penitential rite of the American Roman mass, we, the faithful, 'acknowledge our failures', 'ask the Father's forgiveness', and 'call to mind our sins'. In the Simple Rite of Adult Initiation, the litany before the exorcism contains eight petitions, six of which are specifically about sin and the remaining two which imply it. Thus the faithful, in order to meditate upon their human limits, are asked to recall infractions of God's law. The current practice of abstracting sins implied in the Sunday lessons and so composing the petitions of a penitential kyrie is another example of human limitation being construed as sin because of sins. All this occurs, by the way, with little or no attempt to contrast the Torah with Paul's radical Christian ethic in Galatians.

Perhaps this worked better in a simpler age. People went to confession both because they respected Church authority in a more literal manner than at present and because having been catechised on a single set of morals, they genuinely felt guilty over infractions and sought release from their guilty conscience through forgiveness of their sins. Now that we know a good deal about the history of ethics and are aware of diverse ethical systems, it is nearly impossible for a group of contemporary people to agree on absolute moral positions. The current Christian debates over the nature and moral implications of homosexuality or of abortion demonstrate the monumental disagreements coexisting in contemporary Christian ethics. Some of the most thoughtful Christian ethicists are the ones least sure of *moral absolutes*.

To the extent that sin has become identified with a list of sins, and to the extent that I can receive opposite pastoral counsel as to whether a specific human act is a sin, I will not know whether to confess to God. If I feel guilty, I will not know whether that is my mother's voice nagging me or God's word speaking to me. If I do not feel guilty, I probably do not judge myself guilty, and will not confess. I cannot trust my feelings of guilt or of freedom; I cannot evaluate moral behaviour before God and the community. Our time is a moral free-for-all. The Holocaust is not the exception but the paradigm of a century of moral anarchy. There is no longer in the culture or in the Church a *relatively undisputed moral authority*. For example, a growing number of Christians believe that couples living together before marriage is a healthy social experiment parallel to first vows in monastic life. What do we say? Is this phenomenon an instance of rank immorality, or is it a cultural adaptation of courting rituals which, like any human behaviour pattern, can serve us either toward good or ill? It is ironic that while the Western search for self-awareness developed in tandem with a high consciousness of sin, that search has brought us to a time of acute self-awareness yet a diminished, if not nonexistent, consensus about sin.

3. THE MANY IMAGES OF HUMAN LIMITATION

However, sin is not the only Western Christian image of human limitation, and this fact must inform our panic over the confusion with sin and sins. One alternate image for human limitation is *mortality*. Like sin, mortality has its own history of use in the tradition. *God is God because God creates life* and has life forever, and human limitation is manifested in that we must die. The Genesis story says that the angel guards the tree of life from Adam and Eve so that they may not eat and live forever, and the Scriptures' move toward the Apocalypse brings the faithful back to the tree of life, that they may finally eat and live. The covenant with Noah is a promise for life against death. The hope of the patriarchs for a son is a hope for life in the face of death. Abraham was not concerned about sin and forgiveness: he wanted a son before he died. One interpretation of the incarnation is that God by living and dying as a human being alters our despair over death. By joining us in death, God gives life to death. The resurrection of Jesus is a literal response to our primordial terror of death: we too like Christ will live again. It is true that Christian theology has often interpreted the meaning of the resurrection as the forgiveness of sins. But in the first place, prior to interpretation, the resurrection as an image is part of a complex about life and death, eternal life conquering death, a new life after death. John 3 uses the image of our being born again to new life. The

Orthodox emphasis on deification develops this image: God became human so that we can become divine, thereby conquering mortality. The Paschal vigil is based on the image of life conquering death, and its repeated reference to baptism is not about forgiveness of sin but new life. Current experiments in feminine imagery for God develop the image of death and birth to life, the crucifixion not as forgiveness of sins but as the labour pains toward new life.

A third significant image for human limitation throughout the tradition has been *injustice*. In the narrative of the Exodus, evil was the outside oppressor, and God was the *liberator*. The title of Messiah reflects this metaphor, for in the reign of the anointed one the just would be vindicated and external evil overcome. This image is especially corporate, for God will save a whole people from all its outside enemies. Apocalyticism exemplifies this image: the anti-Christ is out there in the world, and hope for the future lies not in self-criticism or in resurrection but in liberation from those evil regimes. The woman in Revelation 12 is bearing the personification of justice into an evil world. In that the primitive Church speculated whether or how much one sinned after baptism, this image was the operative model. Liberation theologies rely on this language: radical Marxist, Black, and feminist theologies see the greatest human limitation in the systemic evil of which the inside group is relatively innocent and against which the freed faithful are rallied in order to spread God's liberation. Baptism which grants Christian freedom is thus pictured as an anointing to overcome injustice in the world. The intercessions in the eucharistic liturgy demonstrate the whole Church's belief that God has the power to effect justice in the world and so demonstrate divine dominion. The Jehovah's Witnesses are a sect for which this image of injustice has become essential.

There are obvious pastoral problems in designing rituals for a Church in which *some people resonate to the sin/forgiveness image and others to the injustice/justice image.* The sin/forgiveness image urges self-criticism and constructs litanies of self-evaluation. It cultivates and even requires the self-reflective consciousness. (Thus arose the notion that children must be of the age of moral consciousness before they can commune.) However, those who live by the injustice/justice language see this first group as comfortably religious, contented to play out a ritual game of confession and forgiveness while ignoring the massive problems of the poor and the oppressed. The passion of liberation theologies to free society's slaves cannot find assurance in self-contained interior monologues and ridicules this addiction to sorrow and obsessive flagellation. Yet those confessing their sin will judge the liberators as in their own way comfortably self-serving, easily excusing themselves from sin. There will likely be in fact direct conflict in which an action labelled sin by the first group will be lauded as liberation by the second.

Yet the two images must stand in tension. Even in the Scriptures these two images coexist. When the one who forgives sins is named Messiah, forgiveness and liberation have met in Christ.

A fourth image for human limitation is *disease*. This image tends to be used in a highly individualistic manner. The psalms which plead or praise for healing are cast in the first person singular. Although this image has not been prominent in mainline theology, we must admit that the majority of stories about Jesus are of a *healer*. The lepers are cleansed, the blind receive their sight. The etymology of the title Saviour connotes physical healing. Faith healing has been periodically in the Church a popular image of what salvation is, and miracles of healing have been lauded as signs of God's power in the saints. Because of the psychological movement, disease/wholeness has become an increasingly significant image in the twentieth century. Racks of paperback books, weekend retreats, services of healing, and a revival of the rites of anointing demonstrate this image of disease/wholeness in action. Henri Nouwen's enormous appeal attests to the resonance of this language in our time.

A fifth image for human limitation is *meaninglessness*. Before God ordered the universe there was *tohuwabohu*, meaningless chaos. The narratives which tell of the call of the prophets indicate a vision of life in which focus and meaning for human endeavour come from the word of God. Lady Wisdom expressed the Hebrew's hope for beauty and order in chaos. The title of Logos sees in Christ the answer to the human search for meaning: in Christ is word, divine reason, order, meaning. The story of the slaughter of the innocents places Christ within the chaos of human history not as a solution to this meaninglessness but as Emmanuel, God with us. In such a Christology, God becomes incarnate to join us in our meaningless existence and so accompany our struggle for purpose. In Mark's gospel the only cry of Jesus on the cross is his agony of abandonment by God, and in John's gospel, when Philip asks to see God in order to be satisfied, Jesus points to his own life among them. Many modern people are not obsessed by sin, afraid of death, overwhelmed by injustice, or racked by disease; but they are *desperate for meaning*. Christian existentialism offers a sophisticated expression of this image. We cannot be certain whether there is any absolute truth, any ultimate meaning, in life. Like Job, we are baffled by the suffering of the innocent, and we doubt the answers we have been led to believe. Within the chaos we join hands with those who believe in a God who in Christ joined us in human meaninglessness, who offers us a community with which to stride into the future in the faith of realised beauty and order at the end of time. How can we know that the meanings we assume do in fact obtain? Where is Logos in *tohuwabohu*? With this quest for meaning as the dominant image, liturgy is understood as ritual action which begins each week under the paradoxical sign of the cross by ordering chaos into beauty, hospitality, and faith.

4. THEOLOGICAL AND LITURGICAL DEVELOPMENT

No doubt there are *yet other images* for soteriology beyond these five: sin/forgiveness, death/life, injustice/justice, disease/wholeness, chaos/meaning. We have already touched on some of the consequences of this variety of images. Let us quickly rehearse these implications: *It is ignorant to act as if one of these systems is the only orthodox Christian system.* It is myopic to maintain any one image to the absolute exclusion of the others. It is fruitless to attempt to offer a solution from one set to people who understand life under a different set. It is difficult to construct pastoral rituals which are mutually beneficial to people within different systems. It is likely that one's predilection for any one image is a result of one's life experience. It is tempting for any one image even when consciously and conscientiously maintained to become narrowly self-serving.

Awareness of the relative nature of the image of sin and forgiveness suggests to us many disturbing questions. Why has sin become the dominant Western category for human limitation? Ought sin/forgiveness remain paramount? How much do theologians wish to grant partial or full legitimacy to one of the other images? Do the truths articulated by liberation and feminist theologies and the insights explored by psychology and philosophy warrant liturgical rituals in their own language? What is the relation of Christ to human limits as variously described? Which images of God correspond to each image of human need? Ought we try to maintain several or all of the images in order to benefit from the varied expression of truth? How do we individually or corporately profit by our favourite image? How many such systems can a person simultaneously maintain? What is the God beyond our chosen set of images? Which images can most clearly speak grace in our time? How can we train our preachers to ask these questions before they compose their sermons? Undoubtedly there are more questions: this is enough for now!

There is little integrity in urging contemporary people to confess their sin if we cannot defend our answers to at least some of these questions. *In the Scriptures the images overlap in Christ*, and our growing realisation that the God of Christ must be bigger than the Western self-reflective consciousness as articulated by the sin/forgiveness image must make us open to these and other images. We need articulated Christologies and explications of soteriology which develop these significant images for human existence upon which to base liturgical formulas. For the people need the images true enough to their experience and deep enough in the Christian tradition that they may have the foundational language upon which to base their lives. The confessional box may be vanishing, but we do not know what all to put in its place. Its replacement by a pleasantly appointed counselling office has not struggled fully with the complex depths of the problem.

In judging from among images for human limitation, there is yet another criterion. *Knowing human limits ought to be a comfort.* We learn from the transparent honesty of children, and we come to know in the critical decisions of adult life, that limits are good and wholesome gifts of truth. The railing on the crib, the rules of hopscotch, social etiquette, ethical restrictions, the embrace of the lover, the facts from the oncologist, the dirt on the coffin, are in fact limits which keep us from the anguish, forlornness, and despair of ultimate Sartrian freedom. *Human creativity flourishes within bounds*: we must then know those bounds. In ancient myth, humans who were granted eternal life always came to rue it: we welcome limits as a closure to licence. We must then ask which images of human limitation do contemporary people hear with relief, even with joy. To which images do we say a sad and happy Amen, being turned by such a God from such a limitation with delight? Human limitation so articulated would be good news indeed, and we people would flock to hear the words embrace us in our need. The image must be such that it can convey transforming grace. For human life will not escape the limitations: our only hope is that God can transform us within those limits, and, as W. H. Auden wrote, 'In the prison of his days, teach the free man how to praise'.

Finally there is *gratitude for the diversity of images.* Even in the Apostles' Creed the divine life of Christ in the Spirit is expressed in a variety of images: the holy catholic Church, the communion of saints, the forgiveness of sins, the resurrection of the body, and life everlasting. Here God's Spirit is pictured as an ordering of human chaos, a model of justice in the world, our final return to wholeness, and the overcoming of death, as well as the forgiveness of sins. Christ is Forgiveness, Resurrection, Messiah, Saviour, Logos. The task of the liturgist is to find the images which best proclaim the mystery of the Gospel in the vernacular to a living people, and this endless endeavour requires of us the study of both the biblical and traditional Christian images and also the contemporary categories of human need. Perhaps the more images, the better.

Catherine Dooley

The 1983 Synod of Bishops and the 'Crisis of Confession'

MANY AUTHORS acknowledge that there is a *crisis in the sacrament of penance today*. Perhaps it is more accurate to speak about a 'crisis of confession' since the sacrament has been almost exclusively identified with confession of sins since the middle ages. The 1983 World Synod of Bishops on Reconciliation and Penance recognised and discussed the crisis of confession from many different perspectives in the various stages of the synod proceedings. A major issue that surfaced repeatedly in the interventions and discussion is the *relationship of confession of sin to the sacrament of penance* and ultimately to the Church's ministry of reconciliation in the world. With regard to the confession of sin, the synod reaffirmed integral and individual confession with individual absolution as 'the only ordinary means by which the faithful conscious of grave sin are reconciled with God and with the church'.[1] In the synod process, however, this affirmation was drawn from several points of reference. It is the purpose of this article to identify these points, and trace the steps that led to the synod's teaching on individual confession and absolution.

The synod has *three distinct stages*: preparatory, the assembly itself and the post-synod papal exhortation. The process moves from a broad spectrum of concerns and issues to a more focused series of statements; from the involvement of a large number of people to the small Council of the General Secretariat and finally, to the pope himself for the final statement.[2]

In its origins the synod of bishops, an outgrowth of Vatican II, clearly embodied the concept of collegiality. As the synods began to be held triennially, a more structured process was introduced to deal with the number

11

and diversity of issues contributed by the bishop's conferences around the world. Although only a few elected delegates represented each of the various national conferences of bishops at the synod, the entire episcopal group and their constituencies discussed and reacted to the preliminary outline (*lineamenta*) prepared by the Council of the Synod Secretariat in 1982. Their reactions formed the content of a working paper (*instrumentum laboris*) that became the basis of the bishop's interventions and small group discussions (*circuli minores*). The recommendations (*propositiones*) resulting from these discussions were submitted to the pope for consideration and with a view to the preparation of the final document. This essay will examine the synod documents for the understanding of confession of sins in order to see the implications for the 'fate of confession'.

1. PRELIMINARY DOCUMENTS

(a) *Instrumentum laboris*

The working paper for the synod, 'Reconciliation and Penance in the Mission of the Church',[3] placed the sacrament of penance *within the context of an alienated world in need of reconciliation* (part one). The document presents sin as the source of alienation and personal conversion as the necessary means to overcome division (part two). The Church's mission is to be a source and a locus of penance and reconciliation (part three). The *Instrumentum laboris* contains several perspectives on confession of sins. This section on individual confession (n. 35) begins with an exposition of God's initiative toward the sinner and speaks of a gradual and progressive repentance and conversion. It identifies confession of sins as only one of the parts of the whole process of conversion and reconciliation. The document then shifts to the necessity of individual confession and to the role of the priest in sacramental confession. According to the document, the primary reason for confession of sins is that the minister 'must know the sin to be remitted to enable him to decide if he should remit it or not' (n. 35). In the emphasis on the role of the ministerial priesthood, the participation of the ecclesial community in the process of conversion is noted as being helpful but 'conversion is a particularly profound inward act in which the individual cannot be replaced by others and cannot make the community a substitute for him' (n. 35). Moreover, in defining the practice of individual confession, 'the Church is defending the human soul's individual right', which is the right to a more personal encounter with Christ through the minister of the sacrament of reconciliation.

The need for a private, individualised confession and the role of the ministerial priesthood in this section on individual confession of the *Instrumentum laboris* will be underlying themes, directly or indirectly, throughout the synod proceedings.

(b) Report of the International Theological Commission[4]

The International Theological Commission, although not a part of the synod, was asked to prepare a study paper on penance and reconciliation for the 1983 world synod of bishops. The report, however, seems to have had little influence on the synod proceedings. It begins with the anthropological and theological context of conversion and in contrast to the synod working paper, affirms that *because* conversion is a personal act it also has a social dimension. *Conversion to God is irrevocably connected with conversion to one's brothers and sisters.* The report maintains that a balance of both objective and subjective aspects of penance needs to be restored. It is for this reason that the ITC says that a thorough knowledge of the history of the sacrament is required. The historical framework of this report is one of its most important contributions, particularly since the working paper and most of the other documents tend to use historical references as 'proof-texts' or to interpret the past in terms of current practice without regard to the historical context.

The ITC report lists *certain historical non-variables*. The essence of the sacrament is that reconciliation of the sinner takes place by reconciliation with the Church. Both the personal acts of the penitent and the action of the ecclesial community under the direction of the bishops constitute the sacrament.

Variables in the historical development include the diversity in the forms of penance that correspond to the different situations of the Christian life. The changes in sacramental practice are also variables: from once in a lifetime to a repeatable sacrament; from imposition of severe penances to lighter ones; from reconciliation reserved primarily to the bishop to absolution by the priest. Moreover, historical factors determined the overemphasis given to one of the elements of the sacrament that resulted in an deemphasis of other aspects.

The commission concluded that the parts of penance—confession, contrition and satisfaction—must once again be considered in their intrinsic relationship. No one element should be exclusively emphasised. The history of penance shows that a variety of forms of forgiveness are a part of the tradition and need to become again part of the pastoral practice. *A plurality of forms* strengthens the effectiveness of the sacrament of penance.

The ITC report addressed confession of sin from two perspectives. From the anthropological standpoint, the confession of sin, which is the naming of sinfulness and the accepting of responsibility for it, has a liberating and reconciling effect. It enables the person to be free of the past and open to the future. From a theological standpoint, the confession of sin is an aspect of reconciliation. It is part of the process of conversion which has both personal and social dimensions. As the early Church demonstrated, reconciliation with the community is the sign of reconciliation with God.

2. THE ASSEMBLY OF BISHOPS

(a) Homily of Pope John Paul II—29 September 1983

At the Mass opening the 1983 synod,[5] Pope John Paul II reminded the bishops that as successors of the apostles they have particular responsibility for the mystery of the reconciliation of humankind with God. This involves a special 'responsibility for the sacrament in which this reconciliation is completed'. With regard to the confession of sin, the pope noted that confession liberates. When confession born of repentance is united to Christ in the sacrament of reconciliation, it brings about victory over evil. Again, the concern for the sacrament as the means of reconciliation is evident.

(b) Interventions of the Bishops[6]

The bishops' statements—both oral and written—reflect the *diversity of their cultural situations*[7] and a pastoral rather than dogmatic orientation to issues. The practice of individual confession was affirmed and the rationale was primarily drawn from an anthropological basis. Confession of sinfulness is an *acceptance of personal responsibility* as opposed to the temptation of generalisation and collective guilt prevalent in contemporary times. Confession is a painful but liberating act that brings inner healing. It is necessary to reveal the sin in order to be healed. Verbal expression of guilt is important in order to re-evoke past acts in a conscious, orderly and concrete way and so to examine, evaluate and correct them.[8]

The bishops presented different views as to how confession of sins should take place. Many of the delegates, particularly from 'missionary' countries, insisted on the usefulness and necessity of *general absolution*. Some bishops questioned the need for the penitent in serious sin to make an individual confession at a later time. Others questioned whether the Church is not expecting too much from a single rite. Is the same rite appropriate for the *confession of serious sin and for the confession of devotion*? Some suggested that new forms be created.

Other interventions advocated the full implementation of the revised rite of penance with a balanced use of its three existing forms; still others, encouraged the practice of confession as it had been prior to Vatican II.

Several of the South American bishops recommended the restoration of the practice of 'confession to laity' and asked for clear theoretical and practical norms for the role of the lay person as minister of non-sacramental penance. It was noted that many persons—doctors, nurses, pastoral assistants, leaders of basic communities, religious leaders—already fulfill this role and it should be acknowledged.

The bishops' pastoral concerns varied widely and their proposals were too diverse and tentative to suggest a clear focus or plan of action. The very process of the synod demands that the initial contributions of the episcopal conference be reduced to a series of brief interventions that 'barely resemble the complexity of the initial phases of the entire process'.[9] Nevertheless, these brief interventions (eight minutes each and timed by an electric clock!) reflect the *mosaic of situations*, experiences and problems faced by the bishops of various continents, races and cultures.

The interventions occupied the first two weeks of the synod, and then it fell to cardinal Martini in his capacity as relator to summarise the 176 oral and 54 written interventions. It was his task to identify the major issues that had emerged from the interventions and that were to be discussed more thoroughly in small groups during the next phase of the process.[10] The cardinal focused on the rapid decline in individual penance and outlined the three levels of concern for the future of the sacrament of penance: the level of theological investigations of themes, such as the nature and structure of penance and the meaning of sin; the level of celebration, particularly the rite of general absolution; and the image of the Church as the sign of reconciliation.

Joseph cardinal Ratzinger as Prefect of the Sacred Congregation for the Doctrine of Faith had discussed the question of general absolution at an earlier session of the synod.[11] (44(807) 31 October 1983, p. 6.) Cardinal Ratzinger presented two questions for consideration: Is it necessary to confess serious sins already absolved (in the case of general absolution), and is personal confession an essential element of the sacrament? The cardinal stated that the Council of Trent clearly defined that personal confession is an essential element of the sacrament and thus it is necessary to confess serious sin already absolved. Ratzinger remarked that each sacrament must be received personally since sacraments are given to a specific person, not to a group.

Cardinal Ratzinger noted further that absolution has both juridical and therapeutic aspects. Sin wounds not only the person but also society. In confessing one's sins, the individual breaks out of selfish isolation and acknowledges relationship to God and others. Ratzinger concluded that only personal confession is a truly social action. He adds that although there is a need to find more adequate forms for the celebration of the sacrament, the remedy for the crisis does not lie in recourse to general absolution because that encourages trends of depression and of collectivism.

(c) *Circuli minores* and *Propositiones*

The next stage of the process was the *discussion of issues in small groups.*[12] The twelve groups organised according to language focused their discussion around the points suggested by cardinal Martini so that the topics included the notion of sin, general absolution, formation of ministers, and the prophetic ministry of the Church. Many of the groups discussed the 'essentially personal nature of sin' recognising that *social sin results from and leads to an individual's sins.* Sin, as a personal act, is made objective in the social context; therefore, personal and social cannot be so easily distinguished. Confession of sin was seen as a visible sign of inner conversion. Both general absolution and individual confession were affirmed. Three groups spoke for the creation of a lay ministry of reconciliation, not as an alternative but as a complement to the sacramental ministry of the priest.

The considerations of these groups resulted ultimately in the approval of sixty-three *propositiones* that were submitted to the pope. The full text of the *propositiones* has never been published and therefore, they are known only in the form of a short summary. The summary notes that twenty-one of the conclusions dealt with Church's ministry of reconciliation. Four were concerned with an evaluation of the present situation and the remainder centered on the renewal of the practice of reconciliation and of penance. The bishops affirmed the irreplaceable importance of the sacrament of penance, placing it within the broader context of reconciliation.[13] The last thirteen statements dealt with the various forms of the ministry of reconciliation and the role of others besides the minister.

(d) Statement of the Synod of Bishops—27 October 1983

The month long discussions of the world synod of bishops culminated in a powerful call to the Church to become an effective sign of reconciliation and peace in a world where injustice abounds.[14] The bishops note that it is in the sacrament of reconciliation, especially, that 'we celebrate and receive God's forgiveness and know his healing love'. The statement affirms that the sacrament restores and deepens personal friendship with God and then adds an element the documents seldom connect with the sacrament—the *sacrament frees us for service.* The statement does not explicitly mention the confession of sins but places the sacrament within the broader context of reconciliation in the world. The bishops concentrate on the need to struggle for peace and social justice.

(e) Closing address of Pope John Paul II (28 October 1983)

The closing address of Pope John Paul II to the synod[15] reflected some of the concerns expressed by the bishops in the small group discussions. The pope spoke of penance as continuous conversion. Reconciliation, with God or others, is the fruit of this conversion and in this way, penance and reconciliation are fundamental dimensions of the entire Christian existence. The pope also spoke of the need for reconciliation in the areas of ecumenism, 'non-Christian religions' and particularly in the area of world peace. *Working for peace is an integral part of conversion.*

The need to foster a spirit of conversion and to promote world peace form the elements of a contemporary penitential catechesis that is at the same time a preparation for the sacrament of penance. The pope reaffirms the personal character of the sacrament, 'which does not exclude in any way the social dimension of sin and penance'. The sacrament has a central position in the economy of salvation and a special link with the paschal mystery and with the Church.

The final aspect of Pope John Paul II's homily was an affirmation of the synod of bishops as a 'truly great good' and added that the synod, although consultative, 'carries important ecclesial weight'. Therefore, it is essential 'that the documents which appear after the synod, reflect the communal thought of the synodal assembly and of the pope who presides over it *ex officio*'.

At the first three synods (1967, 1969, 1971) the assembly of bishops itself prepared the final document. In 1974, due to the constraints of time, the bishops decided to *submit the synodal conclusions to the pope as a basis for his consideration and final statement.* The result was a lessening of the importance of the synod event itself and an increasing focus on the final papal document. In the final homily, John Paul II states that the synod is one of the most effective instruments of collegiality but that perhaps the instrument could be improved and collegial responsibility could be expressed even more fully.

(f) Apostolic Exhortation: 'Reconciliation and Penance'

The apostolic exhortation which was published more than a year after the closing of the synod seems *as removed in tone as it is in time.* In contrast with the closing homily that was so sympathic to the concerns of the synod fathers, the exhortation seems to differ both in content and style.

The three major sections of the apostolic exhortation[16] released 11 December 1984, are: reconciliation is the mission of the Church; sin is the cause of alienation; and catechesis and the sacraments are the means of pastoral ministry.

The section on the sacrament of penance (nn. 28–30) gives a clear presentation of the teaching associated with the Council of Trent. The focus is placed on the sacrament as the *tribunal of mercy* (n. 31, II), stating that 'according to the most traditional idea, the sacrament is a kind of judicial action' but that this judgment has a *medicinal character*.[17] Throughout the document, the confession of sin is tied to priestly absolution, not in terms of the relationship between the two as parts of the sacrament of penance but in terms of confession of sin as necessary for forgiveness. The exhortion (n. 32) affirms the first form of the Rite of Penance—individual confession and reconciliation—as a normative and the ordinary way of celebrating the sacrament. The document lists the advantages of individual confession: it provides for personal forgiveness and reconciliation with God by regaining the grace lost by sin; it offers the possibility of spiritual progress; it is a means of discerning one's vocation and it is a way in which one can free oneself from spiritual apathy and religious crisis. The document also recommends the sacramental confession of venial sins because the grace proper to the sacrament has remedial power and removes the roots of sin. The exhortation is concerned about the 'vertical' dimension of reconciliation and states that it takes precedence over the 'horizontal' dimension (n. 7). This section of the document seems to reduce the sacrament to the confession of sin and to reinforce a privatised understanding of relationship with God.

The document is *exhortative in nature* and it is part of the ongoing discussion on penance and reconciliation.

3. CONCLUSION

Those who looked to the synod for resolution of the 'crisis of confession' found themselves *facing the same questions and problems after the event as before*. The failure to achieve a clear focus can be traced in part, to procedures that abort the process at the very point where clarity and direction could be reached. Thus, the process itself and the resulting documents reflected a diversity of points of reference. For some bishops, the Council of Trent furnished the theological basis, for others Vatican Council II served this function. Some emphasised dogmatic positions; others stressed the social and political situations. Many placed the confession of sin in a broad context of a process of conversion and reconciliation; others equated the confession of sins and the sacrament of penance. The effort to maintain tradition and continuity was confronted by the need to respond to the pastoral concerns of local situations and diverse cultures.

The tension created by the varied viewpoints served, however, to *highlight the common goals and understandings* that existed among the bishops of the world. The desire to promote the reconciling mission of the church in all its aspects; to foster a spirit of reconciliation in the awareness and life of the people of God; and to encourage all peoples to strive for peace and justice was evident in the discussions and in many of the interventions. The 1983 synod situated the sacrament of penance in the *context of basic human longings for life, love and freedom* which have their source in God. The sacrament calls the Christian to join the struggle to overcome hatred, alienation and oppression and to make a commitment to build a world of love, peace and justice. By placing the celebration of the sacrament of penance in this broader perspective, confession of sins is understood as an expression of personal conversion of life that is basic to the mission and ministry of reconciliation.

Notes

1. Jozef Tomko 'A Retrospective Look at the 1983 Synod of Bishops' *Osservatore Romano* (OR) (Eng) 52 (815) (27 December 1983) p. 6. This article is an informative summary of the synod.

2. For the development of the synod process, see Joseph A. Selling 'How the Synod Works' in *The Tablet* 237 (3 September 1983) 842–846 and 237 (17 September 1983) 890–893.

3. *Origins* 11 (1982) 565–580.

4. 'Penance and Reconciliation' *Origins* 13 (12 January 1984) 513–524.

5. *Origins* 13 (13 October 1983) 306–308.

6. Summaries of the interventions are found in *OR* (Eng) 41–44 (804–807) (October 1983) and *Origins* 13 (18–22) (1983).

7. Cardinal Martini notes that about six-hundred index cards were used to draw up a sort of analytical index of the points touched upon in the bishops' interventions: *OR* (Eng) 44 (807) (31 October 1983) p. 13.

8. See Tomko, the article cited in note 1, p. 7.

9. J. Grootaers and J. Selling *The 1980 Synod of Bishops 'On the Role of the Family': An Exposition of the Event and an Analysis of its Text* (Leuven University Press 1983) p. 12.

10. *OR* (Eng) 44 (807) (31 October 1983) p. 13.

11. *OR* 44 (807) (31 October 1983) p. 6.

12. The reports of the 12 discussion groups are found in *OR* (Eng) 45 (808) 7 November 1983 pp. 4–6.

13. *Origins* 13 (10 November 1983) 371–373.

14. *Origins* 13 (10 November 1983) 370–371.

15. *Origins* 13 (10 November 1983) 376–379.

16. *Origins* 14 (20 December 1984) 432–458.

17. B. Poschmann states that juridical authority in canonical penance belonged to those invested with responsibility for the community. The purpose was the restoration of the relationship of the individual to the ecclesiastical community. In private penance, the notion of penance as ecclesiastical tribunal was lost and so was the presupposition of ecclesial jurisdiction. The focus was mistakenly placed on the nature of the tribunal as such and on the priest as judge who deals with the individual's relationship only to God and not to the community. 'Die innere Struktur des Busssakraments' *Munchener Theologische Zeitschrift* 1 (1950) 17–18.

Dionisio Borobio

The Tridentine Model of Confession in its Historical Context

THIS STUDY does not set out to study the 'sacrament of penance' in all its aspects, but just *'confession of sins' as one of its main elements*. I propose to deal briefly with the importance given to it and its place in teaching and practice throughout the different stages of its operation, so as to situate it within various penitential structures, but to concentrate above all on the Council of Trent.[1] I shall try to put forward a faithful interpretation of the model of confession established there, and to draw the appropriate conclusions from this. We need to analyse the 'confession' element both positively and comparatively, not only in relation to the various phases and structures in penitential development, but also in relation to the other elements that make up the penitential process: conversion, satisfaction and absolution.

There is no doubt that this is a delicate and important subject: it presents hermeneutical difficulties (its cultural, categoric and sociological aspects being different); it is doctrinally controversial (not in its essence but in its implications) and can produce pastoral conflict (being exalted by some and dismissed by others) ... Furthermore, while it is true that the present crisis affecting the whole concept of penance is not just a crisis of confession, it is also true that oral confession of sins is the aspect of penance most in crisis.

1. CONFESSION WITHIN DIFFERENT STRUCTURES OF PENANCE IN HISTORY

In order to assess the place occupied by confession in the Tridentine model of penance, we need to look at the value and place accorded to confession in

21

the *different models and structures of penance that preceded it*.[2] Structures of penance can be classed by the stress or concentration they place on one or other of its constituent elements (conversion, satisfaction or *actio poenitentiae*, confession and absolution). This becomes the manifestatory and creative expression of the identity between the sacrament's meaning and sign.

(a) The structure of penance from the third to the thirteenth centuries

By this 'structure of penance' I mean that established in the Church in the third century, by Tertullian, with the stress laid on 'works of penance' (*actio poenitentiae, satisfactio, labor* ...), as the most appropriate means for expressing conversion (canonical penance), which kept its structure or order of parts—confession and knowledge of the sin, satisfaction, absolution—though within a variety of forms (canonical or tariff penance) till about the thirteenth century.[3] With regard to the place of confession within this structure, it is interesting that early accounts often use the term *exhomologesis* to refer to penance, including not only confession but also satisfaction and the sum total of acts required for reconciliation in this term.[4] Further, the first stage in this penitential process is clearly recognition of sin on the part of the sinful subject, and knowledge of the sin by a bishop or priest (which could come by confession, public scandal or denunciation) since only thus can the due penance be imposed and accepted.

This knowledge and recognition is not a secondary element but an essential and constitutive one, conditioning the process and setting it in motion—the process consisting of seeking penance (*poenitentiam petere*), giving penance (*poenitentiam dare*) and accepting penance (*poenitentiam accipere*). Alongside this structure with confession being an integral part of the Church's penitential process, there is *evidence of another 'curative' (East) or 'corrective' confession (West)*, which did not form part of the canonical penitential process. As Origen and Clement of Alexandria testify for the Eastern Church, as do the anchorite and cenobite monks, besides ecclesiastical penance there was another form centred on confession-direction of a sinner by a guide called '*kybernetes*' or '*pneumatikos*' (who was not necessarily ordained), whose purpose was to lead to a process of healing or purifying.[5] In the Western Church, there are abundant witnesses to a 'confession for correction' (*correptio*), by which was meant the faithful being subjected by their pastors (bishops or priests) to public or private correction, for the purpose of amendment and full reincorporation into the life of the community, but without the intention of subjecting them to official penance (*ordo poenitentium*), either because of their personal inability to carry this out, or because their sins did not warrant it.[6]

This shows that confession was of great importance from earliest times, both as a constituent act setting the penitential process in motion, and as a complementary means of healing and correction. But in these first centuries, the element of confession was *far from occupying the central place* in the process of penance; it has to be seen as a relative or referent element with respect to the process, and a secondary one compared to the conversion manifested in works of penance.

At the end of the fourth century, *penitential discipline changed* (with the introduction of 'tariff penance'), and a system came into vogue the chief factor of which was the assessment and assignation of a particular penance to each sin, with the possibility of repeating the penitential process.[7] The confession-satisfaction-absolution structure of penance remained, but the changes introduced were major ones, the most decisive of them being the effective concentration of the process on confession, which implied a scaling, cataloguing and measuring of sins, which, as they were confessed, attracted one or another penance. This moral casuistry, with its correspondence in penitential confessionism, is amply illustrated in the *libri poenitentiales* of the period. The texts speak again and again of the meaning, need and obligation of confessing sins, exalting its expiatory virtue through the merit of the shame it involves, which could itself become the expiation of the penance deserved.

(*b*) The structure of 'confession' from the thirteenth century onwards

I call 'structure of confession' that which came to be imposed in the Church from the twelfth or thirteenth century. This, besides the concentration of the acts of the process on oral confession, brought a change of structure which changed the classical order of the acts, by giving *absolution immediately after confession*, leaving the satisfaction to be performed later.[8]

(i) *From the thirteenth century to Trent.* Two factors played a decisive part in this major shift: (α) The theory of oral confession as the normal manifestation of contrition, which allows the intervention of the Church and at the same time sums up and synthesises the penitential works and previous satisfaction (*actio poenitentiae*) in itself (through the shame and effort involved: punishment); (β) the importance given to the *potestas clavis*, which implies the exercise of priestly power through the granting of absolution (previously often forgotten by penitents), thereby guaranteeing the fulness of the sacramental sign, which Scholasticism saw as being made up of 'matter' (*quasi materia* in this case: the acts of the penitent, particularly confession) and 'form'—the absolution by the priest. This produced an *important trans-mutation* of the elements: confession became satisfaction as well, absolution came before the *actio poenitentiae* and 'penances' were placed at the end of the process, relegated to a remedy against the temporal punishment due to sin. Such a transmutation raises various questions: why contrition does not make confession useless and absolution ineffective; why confession, taking the place of satisfaction, does not do away with it; why it is even advisable to confess to a lay person if a priest is not available; why absolution expresses God's forgiveness as well as that of the Church ... In the midst of all this 'confessional exaltation', the fourth Lateran Council (IV, c. 21) came to lay down the precept of an annual confession of all one's sins, together with their circumstances, to a priest, starting at the age of reason; penance began to be defined by confession (the 'sacrament of confession');[9] and theologians began to ask themselves whether this confession was by 'divine law' or 'human precept'.

In this context of changing conceptions and practices, it is clear that confession has taken on an importance and come to play a central role that it did not have in the early centuries of the Church, producing a *'dis-order' within the classical structure of penance*. Yet despite this change, the medieval Church was far from making 'confessional penance' the only possible form of penance. Besides the structure of confession, the structure of penance remained in being, in the form of either 'penitential pilgrimage' or 'solemn public penance'.[10]

Besides these forms, which could not be reduced to confession alone, we should note the continued practice of *general or collective absolutions*, which persisted through the middle ages and, particularly in the Gallican Church, down to the sixteenth century (principally during Lent and on Maundy Thursday).[11] They only disappeared with the Council of Trent, when private confession was imposed as the only form of sacramental penance.

(ii) *From Trent to the present.* Despite the persistence of other forms, private penance, and within this the element of confessing sins orally, came to monopolise the various forms and elements of the celebration of the sacrament. The reasons for this evolution before Trent can be seen in various treatises on penance dating from the fourteenth to sixteenth centuries, such as 'Manuals of pastoral care' (*Manipulus curatorum*), 'Summas for Confessors' or 'Confessionaries' in general use, designed to help priests in confession, examination of consciences, giving penances and excommunicating.[12]

The first reason is undoubtedly simply the *exaltation of confession* as the central element (the *Manipulus* of the Spanish priest Guido de Monte Roteri (1333) picks out no less than sixteen 'qualities' of confession).

The second is the *pastoral role and requirements* laid on priests by confession, which in practice came to be one of their chief tasks. Following the Manuals or Summas for confessors (such as that by Antonino of Florence, *c.* 1459,[13] for example), with the need to single out 'reserved sins' and set special penances for them, forced priests to devote a large part of their ministry to this task. The abundance of sins to distinguish and interrogate penitents on, together with the strict regulation of penance, forced both priests and faithful to make their sprituality revolve around what had become simply the 'sacrament of confession'.

The third reason is the *social function or role* played by confession at this time. Even though I do not think it can be reduced to this function alone,[14] there is no doubt that confession, particularly at this period of history, was a system for regulating behaviour, on the individual and collective levels. The social prominence of the clergy, the obligation to confess once a year and sometimes more often, the importance given to sexual or domestic sins, and to those pertaining to the social and professional spheres, the relating of sin and grace to purgatory, damnation or salvation: all these factors combined to make confession a really effective form of social control on the basis of controlling conscience itself.

This practice had positive results (heightened consciousness of sin, a permanent attitude of contrition, regulation of behaviour in social matters or the sphere of justice) which it is difficult for us to envisage today. But it also had not a few negative results: exaggeration of the multiplicity of sins, legalism and a casuistry designed to exhaust every possible circumstance, the anxiety and even anguish produced in sinners and even confessors through excessive fear of judgment and eternal damnation, the abuse of private masses and indulgences as a means of freeing oneself from the punishment due ... All this led to the rise of various reactions against the criticisms of the current practice of confession, from the denunciations of Erasmus of Rotterdam,[15] to the proposals made for stressing contrition rather than confession by Pedro Martínez de Osma[16] and finally the challenges—with their errors—made by Luther and the other Reformers.[17]

Luther, whose thought evolved through several distinct stages (up to 1520; 1521–2; after 1522), not only criticised confession 'which tormented more than it consoled', but also rejected penance as a sacrament (though somewhat ambiguously), denied the value of the acts of the penitent (contrition, confession and satisfaction) in favour of faith-trust in the merciful forgiveness of God; though recognising the value of and need for private confession, he rejected any obligation to make a general confession based on divine law, still less when it was imposed by a pope.[18] Despite this rejection, the Reformers did not give up all penitential practice, but proposed a 'confession-examination' before receiving communion in order to strengthen and sustain baptismal faith,[19] a 'collective absolution' which included the Confiteor and evangelical absolution,[20] and, in Calvin's case, an 'ecclesiastical discipline' with fraternal correction and sometimes even excommunication.[21]

This teaching and practice provoked reaction and controversy in the Catholic field (Leo X, the Universities and theologians),[22] which was particularly sensitive to anything relating to confession. This led to the formulation of *twelve Articles of Protestant Errors*, which were put forward for discussion at Trent. Four of these summed up their errors with regard to confession and read as follows:

4. Confessionem sacramentalem secretam iuris divini non esse, nec apud antiquos patres ante Concilium Lateranense eius factam fuisse mentionem, sed publicae tantum poenitentiae.

5. Enumerationem peccatorum in confessione non esse necessariam ad illorum remissionem ... nec necessarium esse confiteri omnia peccata mortalia. ...

6. Confessionem omnium peccatorum, quam Ecclesia facienda praecipit, esse impossibilem traditionemque humanam a piis abolendam, neque confitendum esse tempore Quadragesimae.

7. Absolutionem sacerdotis non esse actum iudicialem, sed nudum ministerium pronuntiandi et declarandi ... Immo etiam sine confessione peccatoris sacerdotem eum absolvere posse.[23]

So, the Reformers denied fundamental aspects of a doctrine and practice that had become established and dominant in the Church of the time, and called into question the concept of penance developed theologically in Scholasticism and experienced in practice through private confession. The institution, sacramentality, need (*iure divino*), integrity and judicial character of confession—all aspects peacefully accepted till then—and the 'confessionist' practice they involved, were all rejected, and a new doctrine and practice proposed in their place. It is not surprising that *Trent's reaction* to all this was defensive (of the current teaching and practice), coherent (with classic scholastic interpretation), and dogmatic (affirming the basics with authority). But, just because it was all these, it was *also polarised* (at a particular moment in history), prejudiced (against what it set out to change or reject), and largely closed to new insights (through its concern to hold the line at the time). So we need to *interpret its reaction* in a way that takes account of the stronger dogmatic accent in its canons compared to its chapters, of the nature and force of its expressions compared to how far it committed the Church to their content,[24] and also of the overall historical setting of the place it gave to confession, and its particular view of oral confession related to the other elements of the inner structure of the sacrament.

2. AN INTERPRETATION OF THE TRIDENTINE MODEL OF CONFESSION

At this point, we need to look closely at the texts of the Council (the canons above all) in order to make a rigorous (though necessarily limited) appreciation aimed at: (a) identifying the model of confession put forward, and (b) offering an 'open' interpretation of this model. The main reference point for our commentary will be the great Spanish theologian of Trent, Melchior Cano.

(*a*) Identifying the model of confession

As space forbids collecting here all the sources and arguments from which the texts of Trent were built up, let us concentrate on the basic content of the canons dealing with confession (nos. 6 and 7 in particular, taken *per modum unius*), whose nature can be summed up as follows:

(i) *Confession is necessary*. Faced with Luther's affirmation that private confession is not a sacrament instituted by Christ, and that it is not therefore necessary to practise it, Trent declared that it is necessary for salvation, precisely because it was instituted by Christ (can. 6). The arguments on which the Council fathers based this conclusion are various: post-baptismal mortal sin harms the Church community and so it is not sufficient to confess it to God alone; priests should exercise the *potestas clavis*, and it is not possible for them to do this without confession; without exaggerating the support for confession found in the natural and Mosaic laws, they found the basic support for confession in the Scriptures, above all in John 20:23 (but also in Matt. 16:19 and 18:18), confirmed by the permanent tradition of the Church. This is so because Scripture supposes a logic or dynamic of a judicial-healing nature which necessarily implies confession, since if priests are to judge and heal (*praesides et judices*), they can only do so from a knowledge of the case, which they can only get from personal confession of sins, whatever form this is done in.[25] Therefore, if the power of binding and loosing, retaining and forgiving, stems from Christ, so the need for confessing sins as a normal procedure must also stem from Christ if this power is to be exercised prudently and justly. In this 'instituted necessity', the form is not yet specified: whether confession should be secret or public, since in the words of Melchior Cano: 'Nam publicorum publice fieri confessio potest';[26] nor is it yet decided whether there has to be a listing of sins according to nature and frequency.

(ii) *Full confession*. Canon 7 answered Luther's statement that it was impossible to know and remember all one's sins[27] with the decision that oral confession had to be of each and every mortal sin ... 'even secret ones ... and the circumstances that affect the nature of the sin'. Like the scholastic theologians before them, those of Trent certainly upheld the need for confession to be full. The arguments on which they based this were various: drawn from Scripture (John 20:23), the *magisterium* (canon 21 of the fourth Council of the Lateran), or theology (the judicial concept). The underlying reason, however, was always the same: for judgment or discernment to be true and right, full and fair, a full confession must be made, not a partial or truncated one; it must be of all sins and of their particular circumstances, so that retention or forgiveness can be of all sins in their specificity as sins.[28] According to Melchior Cano, the fulness of confession is an integral part of the need for confession itself: 'Nam ob id tenetur homo integre confiteri quia tenetur confiteri',[29] since if confession is necessary for forgiveness, full confession is equally necessary for a total pardoning of all sins. This does not mean that such completeness necessarily implies a *specific kind* of confession, ordered into kind, number and circumstances of sins (though attention must be paid to what affects the nature of sin); what it does imply is the completeness necessary for a 'healing judgment', for the conversion and salvation of the penitent (Cano).[30] The problem is not in accepting the need for complete confession, but in explaining what constitutes a complete confession, what sins must be confessed and in what manner for the condition of fulness to be fulfilled.[31] One thing at least is clear: the Fathers saw ful-ness of confession originating not in the ecclesial community, but in divine will, in the nature of the sacrament, something that had to be seen in the 'line of development originating with biblical requirements concerning conversion'.

(iii) *Confession 'iure divino'*. Both canons 6 and 7 declare that this necessary and complete confession is 'iure divino': 'confessionem sacramentalem vel institutam vel ad salutem necessariam esse iure divino' (6); 'si quis dixerit ... necessarium non esse iure divino confiteri omnia et singula peccata mortalia' (7); something that Luther definitely denied.[32] There is no space here to enlarge on the various interpretations of this.[33] Suffice to record these basic points:

— The scholastics, at least from St Thomas onwards, speak of *ius divinum* ('quod divinitus promulgatur') in relation to confession.[34]

— The theologians of Trent use the term frequently, but neither in the discussions on the subject, nor in the canons that make use of it, does it seem always to have the same meaning, since there are various degrees attaching to it: what is formally or explicitly revealed; what is implicitly or virtually revealed; what has come into the Church through being held to be a usage or institution handed down from the Apostles; what has been established by General Councils or the Fathers of the Church.[35]

— The proceedings of Trent show that the Fathers, in dealing with confession in general, were unanimous in affirming a 'ius divinum' of the first degree (directly stated in the *potestas clavis*) or at least of the second degree ('bona et formali consequentia').[36]

— With regard to 'full' confession, this is stated to be 'iure divino', but not so much directly affirmed in Scripture as contained in the judicial-healing rationale that makes sacramental confession in general necessary.[37]

— As for the circumstances and details that make for fulness, these are not generally held to be 'iure divino' in the same sense or to the same degree as the previous points; some declared them to be 'ius divinum' in the strict sense, others held them to be 'ius humanum simpliciter'.[38] The foregoing shows that the Fathers at Trent did not always use the expression *iure divino* to signify the same degree or intensity of law, but varied it according to the doctrine to which it was being applied. Using these degrees, they made three basic points: (α) that sacramental confession is necessary as a general principle (first or second degree); (β) that this confession should be full ('bona et formali consequentia' of its internal juridical structure, or second degree); (γ) that this fulness should embrace numbers and circumstances of sins ... (coherent ecclesial clarification).[39] The affirmation of these points is made on the basis of their greater or lesser degree of explicitness in Scripture and Tradition, and the degree to which they have been accepted by theologians and Council Fathers.

(iv) *'Conditioned' confession*. Full confession implies confession of 'all and every mortal sin that can be remembered after a suitable and serious examination of conscience ...' (canon 7). This statement is made to counter article 5 of the errors of the Reformers, who denied the need and even the possibility of remembering and enumerating such a multitude of sins.

The requirement of confessing 'all mortal sins that can be remembered' had been formulated long before, and repeated time and again by theologians and Fathers of the Councils. Nevertheless, such a requirement is not something absolute and mathematically exact; it should not be taken to a point where it conditions the validity of the sacrament, obsesses the minister, or torments the penitent;[40] it should be a more formal, relative requirement: there should be a diligent examination of conscience, but this is conditioned by the physical and moral capability of the subject. Sins forgotten are included in sins confessed (see DS 1680, 1682, 1707).

In fact, theologians and Fathers recognise and state possible exceptions to this obligatory nature, such as when confessing certain sins might be an occasion of scandal, bring danger of death or infamy, or when there is a physical impediment (dumbness, approaching death, unconsciousness, etc.).[41] It is, however, understood that there should be some external manifestation or sign made, so that the discerning-judicial function of the Church can respond.

(v) *Secret confession.* Against the Protestant teaching that secret confession did not exist before the fourth Council of the Lateran, and that it was therefore alien to the institution by Christ,[42] Trent affirmed that 'the method of confessing in secret to a priest alone, such as the Church has practised from the beginning and continues to practice' is not 'alien to the institution and command of Christ' (canon 6). The theologians and Fathers of Trent were not ignorant of the historical existence of other forms of penance, such as public penance, or that this had persisted for a long time.[43] But they opposed all evidence put forward by the Protestant side to show that secret confession had not existed from the beginning; this was consistent with their 'confessionist' view of history.[44] Whatever the rights and wrongs of their case, what they said can be summed up in two parts:

(α) *Confession in secret does not appear to have been explicitly commanded by Christ,* nor is there any indication that Christ forbade public confession (ch. 5, DS 1683), but the former is in line with Christ's institution and command and should therefore be practised, even if such practice cannot be qualified as *de iure divino.* What is *de iure divino* is confession itself, not whether it should be public or secret.[45] Secret confession, far from going against the natural law, is coherent with the very precept of Christ.[46] The Fathers do not condemn public confession, and even ask for it to be retained; what they condemn is the rejection of the coherence and value of private confession. This is what emerges most explicitly from the doctrinal chapter on the subject (DS 1683).

(β) It is stated that this private confession was practised 'from the beginning and always' (canon 6). This statement, while repeated by some theologians and bishops, should not be taken in a strict, but in an implied sense, as the following facts indicate: first, some of the Fathers, such as Archbishop Beccatelli and the Archbishop of Oviedo, asked that 'in 7° deleatur "ab initio" ',[47] while others asked 'deleatur vocalem',[48] which shows a desire to mitigate the statement by making it refer rather to confession in general; secondly, the distinction proposed between confession *cum obligatione* (sacramental) and *sine obligatione* (optional and devotional), showing that the 'semper fuisse in Ecclesia' could refer to both sorts;[49] thirdly, the explicit reference to 500 years before the Lateran Council as a clarification of the phrase 'ab initio semper', as proposed by the Bishop of Orense.[50]

This 'ab initio semper' is something of an exaggeration on the part of Trent, explained by its opposition to the Protestants and its conviction that anything good done by the Church of the time must always have been so. But in fact, private confession in general (whether to lay or ordained people) is one matter, and the practice of private sacramental confession as necessary for penance, or the 'confessional' structure of penance, is another. While the former always existed in one form or another, the latter is a later development. The fourth Council of the Lateran did certainly mark a change in the confessional structure of penance.

(vi) *Confession once a year.* The Reformers denied the obligation to confess once a year, as had been laid down by Lateran IV, canon 21.[51] Trent upheld the obligation and the goodness of this precept and custom (canon 8, DS 1708; ch. 5, DS 1683); while a positive precept, it had pedagogical value and ensured minimum compliance with the general requirement to make confession.[52] This does not mean that the obligation to confess should be restricted to Lent, since there are other times when it is obligatory (in danger of death, before receiving communion ...), and equally the precept can be fulfilled at other times; Lent, however, is the most favourable time for fulfilling the obligation (DS 1683). There is no doubt that this is a human precept, not a divine one, but its pedagogical value, its fulfilling of the precept of confession in general, and its function as preparation for Easter, should all serve to persuade the faithful that they should fulfil their obligation in Lent.[53]

(b) An 'Open' Interpretation of this Model of Confession

The last few years have produced *two opposing interpretations of the Tridentine doctrine on confession,* as can be seen from the latest official documents on penance: *Normae Pastorales, Ordo Poenitentiae,* the new *Code of Canon Law, Ex. Reconciliatio-Poenitentia.*

The first, more narrow and literal, is found chiefly in the stress laid on 'full' confession (above all in the *Code* can, 988, 1), and the (to my mind) not very considered statement that 'individual and full confession ... is the *only normal means* of reconciliation'.[54]

The second, more open and adaptable, without underplaying the value of the Tridentine model of confession, interprets its language in the light of the situation, conception and practice of the time, setting oral confession in the context of the dominant structure of the period, and of the other elements that go to make up the sacrament. There are traces of this approach in the *Ordo Poenitentiae* and in various authors.[55]

Trent devoted a great deal of effort to clarifying the question of penance. The great theologians of penance (above all Cano and Tapper) and the Fathers were well aware of errors, Tradition and Scripture. Their coherence and logic are substantial. Yet, because of the times, because of the current concepts and practice, they could not escape *certain preferences* which led to their going to extremes in some aspects of their interpretation: first, their 'confessionalist' concentration; second, their polarisation of the judicial structure of the sacrament; third, their reduction in the number of forms for its celebration.

(i) *'Confessionalist' concentration.* Oral confession is certainly the commonest, most significant and obvious form of penance. But it only became so through the *diminution of the historical importance of satisfaction, or the removal of the centrality of conversion.* Confession expresses and authenticates, precedes and leads to conversion; as an oral expression, it needs to be complemented with the operational expression of satisfaction. Trent appreciated this mutual correlation and therefore insisted on the three acts (contrition, confession, satisfaction) needed to make up the sacrament. But in fact these elements were not placed in a balanced relationship according to their order of importance, either in doctrine or in practice. Confession alone commanded attention, discussion, decision-making and pastoral concern. The fact that it is not sins alone that are confessed, but also the will to conversion and satisfaction, was largely forgotten.

(ii) *The judicial structure of the sacrament.* Its judicial nature affects the original structural centre of penance itself (binding-loosing, retaining-forgiving). But the image and analogy are sometimes forced—*ad instar judicii*; civil judicial procedures are transposed to the sacramental; there is a lack of integration with *images of healing* (medicine: a process of curing) and *caring* (the shepherd looking for the lost sheep ...), and the nature of penance as process is forgotten in the concentration on a formal judicial act. Of course, penance supposes an intervention on the part of the Church (through a minister) to discern and judge concerning a situation of 'grave' sin that affects the holiness and identity of the believing community. The purpose of this correcting and discerning intervention is to distinguish good from evil and place them in context, so as to draw the penitent out and help him or her to escape from sin and join the communion of grace, through a process of change and conversion, so that the holiness and identity of the Church is safeguarded and guaranteed with the reconciliation and salvation of the sinner in Christ. This discernment or judgment is applied not only to the degree of gravity of the sin, but also to the desire for conversion, to the damage done to the fraternal community, to the actions necessary for reconciliation in penance, so that the process involved in 'binding and loosing' can be fully carried out. Two things are needed for this:

(α) The subject must make sufficient outward indication of his situation of sin (or of what really and subjectively makes him a sinner) and of his desire for conversion, for this intervention and process to come about. Normally, such an indication is given through words (confession) and deeds (satisfaction). The harmonious relationship between the two should not be disturbed by the different possibilities (of time, place, manner) of giving this indication. Neither element (confession or satisfaction) should be regarded as 'independent absolutes'; both are relative to and dependent on conversion and the required intervention by the Church. Therefore, if it could be shown that this intervention and discernment can duly be exercised with some other form of indication that the oral confession now enforced and the form of satisfaction now current—if other signs can be recognised as valid—there would be no difficulty in proclaiming sacramental reconciliation to have taken place. What is basically *de iure divino* is the need for an outer indication of the situation of sin and desire for conversion so that there can be intervention by the Church, healing, reconciliation and forgiveness. Confession and satisfaction, then are *de iure divino* to the extent that they are necessary for such an indication to be made, but not in any particular form.

(β) Intervention and discernment also requires positive action on the part of the Church, which consists not only in 'judging', but also in making the result of the 'judgment' known, showing the penitent what conditions or satisfaction are required (*actio poenitentiae*), and making it possible for them to be carried out through a step by step process of separation (binding) and bringing closer (loosing) culminating in sacramental reconciliation and absolution. Satisfaction includes both desire to heal on the part of the Church (*poenitentiam dare*) and desire for conversion on the part of the sinner (*poenitentiam accipere*). The first step is that of retention by the Church (*ligare, retinere*) followed by the second step of sacramental reconciliation (*solvere*). Now, this 'judicial' understanding, so well expressed in the structure of excommunication or penance, has lost its real meaningfulness in the structure of confession enjoined by Trent, since the place and value given to satisfaction do not express the process described above, and because the meaningfulness lost is not replaced by or adequately expressed in the immediate granting or refusing of absolution.[56] If this meaningfulness is to be recovered, I believe the Church, while retaining the present forms, should also think of renewing the earlier form of penance, called either 'public' or 'solemn' or 'greater' or 'the penitential process', which could be the main form in Lent particularly, and especially for those who consider themselves 'great penitents'.

(iii) This brings us, finally, to the third point on which Trent's solution is somewhat one-sided: *the reduction of forms of penance*. In none of its documents did Trent explicitly state that 'individual and complete confession and absolution are the *only* normal form' of sacramental reconciliation. In practice, however, this is what is understood and what has happened, to the exclusion of other forms current till then, such as 'public penance or penitential pilgrimage', 'solemn Lenten penance', 'absolutory' penance with collective absolution ...

This fact, which was brought about by a positive underlying intention (to promote unity and guard against error), has had *not a few negative results: individualism and privatism, 'confessionism', neglect of the community dimension, undervaluing of other elements of the sacrament* ... Trent has often been made to say more than it did or could have said about forms of penance. But Trent was conscious of and did not reject various possibilities for penance, such as the form involving public confession of sins (DS 1683), public penance imposed for a public sin (decree on Reform, can VIII),[57] penance that expresses the 'binding' function in the way of the early Church,[58] or that supposed by 'reserved' cases (DS 1686). The fact that there has been a reduction of forms since Trent should not be an obstacle to an openness to new forms of sacramental celebration which, by modifying the principle of the '*unicus modus ordinarius*', would have their own place and value in the Christian community, providing they fulfilled the essential and permanent elements of the expressive structure of penance (confession, satisfaction, absolution). Within this proviso there would be (as there always has been throughout history) room for a variety of ways in which these elements could be expressed.

Confession as laid down by Trent does not require one sole form of confession 'in actu' for sacramental celebration to take place. The satisfaction it proposed does not exclude other forms and orders by which satisfaction can be fulfilled. The 'judicial' absolution set out at Trent does not stand in the way of producing a more meaningful explanation of 'binding and loosing'. *So Trent itself provides possibilities of evolution*; for this to take place, we need to look beyond the polarised views of the council itself, and one-sided later interpretations of it, to follow the different strands of penance through history, and through the relationship between its various elements. The problem does not lie with the form of 'confession' established at Trent, but with the claim that this represents the only possible way of celebrating the sacrament of penance.

Translated by Paul Burns

Notes

1. Among the most recent studies on the subject are: Z. Alszeght and M. Flick 'La dottrina tridentina sulla necessità della confessione' in *Magistero e Morale* (Bologna 1970) pp. 101–192; K. J. Becker 'Die Notwendigkeit des vollständigen Bekenntnisses in der Beichte nach den Konzil von Trient' in *Theologie und Philosophie* 47 (1972) 161–228; J. Escudé-Casals *La doctrina de la confesión integra desde el IV Concilio de Letrán hasta el Concilio de Trento* (Barcelona 1967); various *El sacramento de la penitencia: XXX Semana Española de Teología, Madrid 14.5.70* (Madrid 1972); H. Jedin 'La Nécéssité de la confession privée selon le Concile de Trente' in *La Maison-Dieu* 104 (1970) 88–115; P. E. McKeever *The Necessity of Confession for the Sacrament of Penance* (Washington 1953); M. Mancelli *La confessione dei peccati nella dottrine penitenziale del Concilio di Trento* (Bergamo 1966); A. Duval *Les Sacrements au Concile de Trente* (Paris 1985), IV *La Confession* pp. 151–222; A. Amato *I pronunciamenti tridentini sulla necessità della confessione sacramentale nei canone 6–9 de la sessione XIV (25.11.1551)* (Rome 1974).

2. For a fuller account, see D. Borobio 'Estructuras de reconcilación de ayer y de hoy' in *Phase* 128 (1982) 101–125.

3. See the historical investigations of writers such as J. Jungmann, B. Poschmann, K. Rahner, E. Bourque, P. Anciaux, G. Galtier, C. Vogel, H. Karpp ... See D. Borobio *La penitencia en la Iglesia hispánica del s. s. IV–VII* (Bilbao 1978).

4. See J. Mühlsteiger 'Exomologese I' in *Zeit. für Kath. Theol.* 1 (1981) 1–32.

5. See S. Frank 'Fundamentos históricos de nuestra praxis penitencial y confessional' in *Conversión y reconciliación* ed. F. Schlösser and R. Rincón (Madrid 1973) pp. 47–74.

6. I believe this '*correptio*' to have been given not only for '*peccata levia et quotidiana*' but also for more serious sins which did not merit the full rigour of ecclesiastical penance: See D. Borobio *La penitencia* ... cited in note 3, pp. 137–141.

7. See C. Vogel *Le Pécheur et la pénitence au Moyen-Age* (Paris 1969); *idem Les 'libro poenitentiales'* (Turnhout 1978).

8. Besides C. Vogel and B. Poschmann, see P. Anciaux *La Théologie du sacrement de la Pénitence au XIIme siècle* (Louvain-Gembloux 1949).

9. See N. Bériou 'Autour du Latran IV (1215): la naissance de la confession moderne et sa diffusion' in Groupe de la Bussière *Pratiques de la confession* (Paris 1983) pp. 73–92.

10. See Vogel *Le pécheur* ... cited in note 7, p. 34.

11. Two recent studies are: L. Vencser 'Bewertung der Generalabsolution in Lichte der Bussgeschichte' in *Studia Moralia* 15 (1977) 469–482; N. Lemaître 'Pratique et signification de la confession communuataire dans les paroisses au XVIme siècle' in *Pratiques de la confession* cited in note 9, pp. 139–157.

12. See T. N. Tentler *Sin and Confession on the Eve of the Reformation* (Princeton 1977).

13. See P. Michaud-Quantin *Sommes de casuistique et manuels de confession au Moyen-Age (XII–XVI)* (Louvain 1962).

14. See H. Martin 'Confession et contrôle social à la fin du Moyen-Age' in *Pratiques* ... cited in note 9, pp. 117–134.

15. See J. P. Massaut 'La Position oecuménique d'Erasme sur la pénitence' in *Réforme et humanisme* (Montpellier 1975) pp. 260ff.

16. See *J. López de Salamanca and P. Martínez de Osma: La confesión y las indulgencias. Prereforma y tradición* ed. R. Hernández (Salamanca 1978).

17. See L. Klein *Evangelische-lutherische Beichte* (Paderborn 1961).

18. *Martin Luthers Werke. Kritische Gesamtausgabe* (Weimar 1883ff. = WA), in particular here: WA 2, 646, 16ff.; WA 8, 58, 5.

19. See *La Confession d'Augsburg* tr. P. Jundt (Paris-Geneva 1979) art. 25.

20. See Ph. Denis 'Remplacer la confession' in *Pratiques* ... cited in note 9, pp. 165–176.

21. *Letter from Calvin to Fareil*, Strasbourg, 29 Apr. 1540.

22. In his Bull *Exurge Domine* of 15 June 1520 Leo X condemned ten propositions relating to penance (DS 1455063). Among universities, the Sorbonne pronounced in 1535 and 1542, Louvain in 1544. Many theologians wrote on the subject, among them Alonso Castro, Melchior Cano, Diego Laínez, J. Gropper, F. Nausea, R. Tapper.

23. *Concilium Tridentinum. Diariorum, Actorum, Epistularum, Tractatum nova collectio* ed. Societas Goerresiana (Freiburg 1901ff. = CT); here CT VII/1, 234, 8–236, 13.

24. A. Amato *Necessità de la confessione sacramentale* cited in note 1, pp. 82–87, nn. 25–58.

25. Most authorities wield this argument in one form or another, such as Melchior Cano 'Relectio de Poenitentiae sacramento' in *Melchioris Cano Opera* (Madrid 1760) pp. 528ff. Here see p. 575.

26. *Ibid*, VI p. 592. Similarly in CT VII/2 pp. 242, 249, 254, 255, 272.

27. WA 56, 283, 3–7.

28. Thus Melchior Cano in *De Poen. sac.* VI, p. 592: '... Tantum itaque criminum poenitens confessori debet manifestare, quantum opus erit ad salubre poenitentis judicium ... qui enim confessionem instituit, non mancam et mutilam, sed integram instituit. Deo quippe perfecta sunt opera'. See CT VII/1, 261–264.

29. *Ibid.* VI, p. 593.

30. *Ibid.*

31. For Amato, generic confession is in some cases not opposed to this fullness. See *Necessità* ... cited in note 1, p. 200.

32. WA 2, 645, 16.

33. See K. Rahner 'Über den Begriff des Jus divinum in katholischen Verständnis' in *Schrift. für theol.* V (1962) 249–277.

34. St Thomas *Summa Theol.* 2a, 2ae, q 57, a. 2 ad 3.

35. G. A. Delfino distinguished three degrees: explicit, implicit and statutes or councils: CT VI/1, 70, 17–23. Monastic theologians, on the other hand distinguish four: CT VI/2, 47, 20–38.

36. CT VII/1, 308, 18–21.

37. Melchior Cano *De Poen. sac.* VI, p. 593 expresses it thus: 'Pro huius rei explicatione, cum primis advertendum est, unum idemque praeceptum esse de

confessione, de ejus integritate, de examine conscientiae, ac praeceptum inquisitione. Nam ob id tenetur homo integre confiteri, quia tenetur confiteri, et idcirco examinare conscientiam, et peccata, quae fecit, inquirere, quia debet integritatem in confessione servare'.

38. Thus M. Olabe: CT VII/1, 264, 43–45. And Delfino: CT VI/2, 48, 26–49.

39. I would in general agree with A. Amato that ch. 7 speaks of 'divine law' in the latent sense: see the work cited in note 1, pp. 178, 199–200.

40. This is Luther's accusation: WA 6, 161–164, 8; CT VI/1, 51, 10, 19–20.

41. Melchior Cano himself recalls this: De Poen. sac. VI, pp. 590–600ff.

42. CT VII/1, 234, 7–10.

43. Cano, ibid. VI, p. 592. Cf CT VI/1, 69, 3106.

44. A. Duval Les Sacrements ... the work cited in note 1, pp. 185–194.

45. In the general congregation of 14 Nov. 1551, Bishop Egidio Foscarario said: 'Christus autem confessionem in genere instituit, modum vero, quod fiat secreta vel publica, non instituit; utroque igitur modo fieri potest, et utroque modo Christi praecepto satisfit': CT VII/1, 319, 13–15.

46. Thus Tapper: CT VII/1, 249, 28–32.

47. CT VII/1, 329, 21; 331, 7–8.

48. CT VII/1 329, 5; 328, 28; 330, 25; 331, 15–16.

49. CT VI/1, 56–57.

50. CT VII/1, 307, 10–12.

51. WA 6, 162, 22–26.

52. Cano De Poen. sac. VI p. 628.

53. See CT VI/1, 260, 21–25; 269, 39; 274, 23–25.

54. This statement, absent as such from Trent, seems to me to suppose a major reduction in interpretation of the forms, which certainly did not come about till post-Trent practice. The first document to use the expression is the Normae pastorales, I: 'Individualis et integra confessio atque absolutio manet unicus modus ordinarius, quo fideles se cum Deo et Ecclesia reconciliant, nisi impossibilitas phisica vel moralis ab huiusmodi confessione excuset': AAS 64 (1972) 511, taken up again in OP 31; Codex ... , can. 960.

55. See D. Borobio 'Sacramental forgiveness of Sins' in Concilium 184 (1986) pp. 95–112.

56. On this point see recent articles by B. de Margerie 'La Mission sacerdotal de retenir les péchés en liant les pécheurs. I. Interêt actuel et justification historique d'une exégèse tridentine' in Revue de Sciences religieuses 4 (1984) 300–317; 'II. L'Exégèse médiévale. Le pouvoir de lier les pécheurs en retenant leurs péchés' in ibid. 1 (1985) 35–50; 'III. Luther et Trente face au pouvoir de lier et de retenir' in ibid. 2 (1985) 119–146.

57. Conc. Oecumenicorum Decreta ed. G. Alberigo (Rome 1962) pp. 11, 27–39.

58. DS 1692.

PART II

Pastoral Issues

Konrad Baumgartner

The Process of Conversion and its Ministries

> Come, let us return to the Lord;
> He has torn us,
> He will also heal us ...
> After two days he gives back our life.
> On the third day he raises us up.
> And we live before him
> > (Hos. 6.1).

1. THE NATURE OF CHRISTIAN CONVERSION

CONVERSION AND FAITH—that has always been the Christian's fundamental response to the Gospel, in the past as now: conversion in free assent, as personal act, sustained by the community of the Church. In conversion everyone is addressed in a different way, but the question with which we are confronted is always the same: are you prepared to *forgo the self-confident shaping of your own history*, and God's history with us? Are you ready to trust the joyful message that God has come into our world, and to surrender yourself entirely to this message (P. Hoffmann's words)?

Metanoia—conversion, repentance—means a change of mind which refashions the whole of existence. It is a radical, limitless and *unconditional re-poling of life* which makes Jesus Christ the compass point by which and towards which we steer. These new bearings find their concrete and concentrated realisation in the sacraments and ministries of the Church. For

41

Christians, the centre of gravity is not their own self-centredness, their own interests, or salvation through their own efforts. The gravitation that moves them is the truth and love revealed to us in Christ. So, as L. Schwarz says, conversion means responding to the assurance that God has chosen us, turning wholly to him and his task for us in the world, and turning away from all other forces. Conversion therefore brings about a radical change in the Christian's identity. The old godless way of living, and the old understanding of what we are ('a person is his own salvation'—*solus homo salus*) have to be replaced by a new practice of living, by a new understanding of what we are, here and now, in the face of the new questions cast up by 'the signs of the time' in their macro and micro-structures.

Conversion implies a *turning back*: a turning back from false and unworthy ideas about human beings, as well as from practices which are an attempt to dispose over God—from mere ritual penance, from a religion of 'works', and from a legalistic superintendance and administration of conversion. Positively speaking, conversion means turning to Jesus and making a total decision for him who, as R. Schulte puts it, 'brings judgment as grace, and grace as salutary judgment'. Jesus has given conversion a new face. God is a God who does not so much require penance and observance of 'the law', but who gives forgiveness freely and for nothing, and expects faith in return. 'It is not of him ... that runneth, but of God that sheweth mercy' (Rom. 9:16 AV): the main emphasis is no longer on our own exertions and our own 'running'. The centre is God's loving compassion and the appropriate response to it. For the decisive turn has been made by God himself, in Jesus Christ, in the paschal mystery which is the central *metanoia* event for the world. But this *metanoia* event is to be mediated into the midst of history *through the Church*. The Church becomes a person's way into the reality of the reconciled relationship between God and human beings first of all, but also between human beings themselves. Through the Church God desires to turn men and women to himself again, and with them the whole universe, redeeming and saving them, bringing them to a full, comprehensive and enduring life together with him. As *conversi*—those who have been converted and redeemed—Christians are intended to be co-workers in this divine *metanoia*—action in the world and for the world. The community between them and in which they live is itself to be *sacramentum mundi*, the sign and instrument, the model that is already the event of a new life among human beings, a life with one another and for one another, a community grounded in Jesus Christ which makes him its yardstick. This requires Christians themselves to practise 'a culture of conversion' and a 'pastoral ministry of conversion'.

It is part of the provisional and fractured nature of human existence—and Christian existence too—that the reality of conversion only exists among

Christians *in germ*. Jesus' question is still: 'Don't you understand? How difficult it is for you to believe all this!' (see Luke 24:25). For although conversion is the gift of God, it is none the less what P. M. Zulehner calls 'an event with a human face'. A person's originally sinful existence puts up resistance and defends itself; the promises of the world are too fascinating, the life-style built up on power, achievement and society's standards is too dominant for us to allow ourselves to be ruled by the crucified love of God, by the hierarchy of humility and the option of non-violence. Moreover many pious people are religious but not believing. For them God and religious practices are protective securities. They keep God and his demand for conversion at arm's length. They do not dare to surrender themselves with ultimate consistency to God and Jesus' way of life. For becoming a Christian is about a change in the person himself, not merely at one or another point but, as J. Ratzinger says, without reservation, down to the ultimate ground of his being.

Perhaps this halving of *metanoia* is the real reason for the crisis in Christianity today. We need decisiveness and consistency in our adoption of 'the new way'.

2. CONVERSION AS PATH AND PROGRESS

(*a*) The 'Journey' Character of Conversion

It is no contradiction of all this to say that we have to see conversion as a *journey*, a path with ups and downs, detours and dead-ends, with waterless deserts and weary stages. The first name for Christians was probably 'people of the new way'. This is still true, even if the term itself has disappeared. Before Easter this path meant discipleship of Jesus according to the traditional Greek and Jewish conversion pattern (renunciation of all possessions, being hated, leaving one's relations behind). This discipleship reflects the transition from being a Jew (or gentile) to being someone who confesses Jesus. In the light of the imminent kingdom of God, discipleship of Jesus is defined as eschatological *metanoia*, as conversion in the truest sense. 'The *metanoia* required by the coming kingdom of God is conversion to Jesus', says E. Schillebeeckx. This *complete orientation towards Jesus* among the people who accompanied and followed him before Easter is the model of what, after Easter, Christian life simply has to be. It is therefore quite correct to talk about faith before Easter as being 'faith in the process of becoming'. The Easter experience, the confrontation with Jesus' passion, and the encounter with the risen Lord give conversion a new quality: they lead to conversion to Jesus in its post-Easter form, *confession of the crucified and now risen Christ*.

Will it be permissible to conclude from this that being a Christian—which always means becoming a Christian—involves *conversion in two stages, one 'before Easter' and one 'after'*? Can we therefore talk about a 'first' and a 'second' conversion? The first conversion means the *'yes' of faith to baptism*, whether that 'yes' precedes baptism or follows it. Without drawing on this faith in Christ in everyday life—turn the cheque into current coin, as it were— the person who has been baptised (as infant) is really someone who, though baptised, is unconverted. By no means a few Christians are in just this state. In spite of the fact of baptism, they have really not yet arrived at their first conversion. They have not (yet) given an assent of faith, in a conscious and personal act, 'to the God of revelation, who has shown us his face in Christ' (H. Schürmann's words). The *deliberate 'yes' to Jesus*, and an assenting acceptance of his way: this is the heart of the first conversion. It is this to which the Church's proclamation invites men and women, and it is for this that it offers help through its ministry. Today too, just as at the time of Jesus himself, there are plenty of 'Jesus sympathizers', whose interest never develops into a permanent orientation towards Jesus. Even less does it lead these people to join a community of Jesus' disciples. It is difficult, even impossible, to judge the quality of this kind of contact with Jesus.

The Easter experience leads the disciples to the *post-Easter, 'second' conversion*. This is the foundation of the Church and its mission. Discipleship in the form it took before Easter has turned into community with the exalted Jesus, an existential implementation that, as W. Thüsing says, 'coincides with the whole life of believing men and women'. Of course a post-Easter discipleship of this kind is not the closed preserve of the pure and the perfected. On the contrary: it must remain open for processes of growth, in both individuals and groups. It must include the communication of life and faith, as well as, and above all, solidarity with people who are searching. In the deepest sense, the second conversion means a *total surrender of existence, total commitment and total devotion*. It means being fused with Christ, giving oneself up to God in every situation in life. It means renouncing an independent fashioning of one's own future, and handing over the past to God's will, in faith. At this stage the Christian way of conversion will be a path modelled on Jesus' own destiny in death and resurrection: a dying with Christ and a being-risen with him. Consequently Christian martyrdom is the most concentrated and consistent visible form of *metanoia* existence; but the death of every Christian should also reflect an existential acceptance of the paschal mystery of Jesus.

What I have just said is true of the Easter experience of Jesus' disciples. It applies also to Paul's vision on the Damascus road. His 'journeying' from Jerusalem to Damascus already in itself makes this a symbolic conversion story. According to Acts 26:12–18, the Damascus road vision was an Easter appearance which grounded and legitimated Paul's mission as apostle to the gentiles. And it is at the same time an ecclesial 'call' vision, like the appearance to Peter and the eleven. *Conversion and mission, that is to say, are inseparable.* We may say with the Jewish Scholar Schalom Ben-Chorin that Paul experienced himself 'as the place of the theophany where the Son of God revealed himself, so that in fact Christ's resurrection took place (again) in Paul's person'. Or, like Josef Blank, we may put more emphasis on the 'call' aspect, rather than on the conversion—for after all, Paul was not converted from unbelief to belief. He was not an unbeliever, and certainly not an atheist or immoral. What happened to him was conversion 'from the Torah as path of salvation to the Gospel as path of salvation'. But whatever the emphasis, everyone would agree Jesus' death and resurrection became for him the great turning point and mission of his life.

To experience Easter therefore means an intensive conversion, and also a mission that determines the whole of existence. But both these consequences are always theologically embedded in the surrounding ecclesial field. This was as true for Paul (See Acts 9:10–26) as it was for the Emmaus disciples or for Thomas. The *doulos* existence—existence as servant—which took shape in the encounter with the risen Christ is the convert's fundamental Gestalt, or configuration: *to be totally at the Lord's disposal, and to be sent on behalf of men and women.* The two-stage path of conversion is and must be opened up by God himself: as call to the discipleship of Jesus and as encounter with the One crucified, who said of himself: 'I am the Way, the truth and the life' (John 14:6). The invitation to take this path can be given in the astonishing light of a divine revelation, as it was with Paul or Pascal. But it can also overwhelm people in the quietness of everyday life, so that they take 'the little way', like Thérèse of Lisieux. The call can come in the Christmas midnight celebration, as it did to Paul Claudel. Or—like the call to Mother Teresa—it can be a summons to leave the religious community to which one has hitherto belonged, and found a new one.

The Christian path of conversion is therefore linked at its very heart with Christ, as the great turning point—with the Easter mystery which is intended to mould and transform the whole of life (see the collect for the 6th Sunday after Easter). A 'ministry of conversion' must therefore move in two directions. In the first place it must reach out to help people who are face to face with their first conversion. This help can be given through religious instruction, for example, or through preparation for the sacraments, youth work or preaching. But in the second place it must minister to Christians who have come to the point of a second conversion. It can help these people through pastoral counselling, through spiritual exercises and spiritual guidance, especially also in the dialogical sacrament of reconciliation and penance. All these things could be the source of reconciled life: life reconciled with God, with human beings and with creation.

(b) The Process Character of Conversion

Nobody is a Christian once and for all. Everyone continually becomes a Christian anew. Becoming a Christian is an event, a pro-gression, a pro-ceeding, a process. Because of this, becoming a Christian means continually departing from 'stand-points'. 'Becoming a Christian happens on the move', says M. Niggemeyer. Consequently learning to believe should be thought of as the graduated process of a history of faith. What E. Feifel describes as the *'phase structure of the history of faith' corresponds to the phase structure of the human life cycle.*

A person's life does not take a steady linear course. It proceeds in phases or stages. Here every phase has its own significance, in each case presenting new tasks which contribute to growth and maturing. And only when the tasks of a given phase have been mastered is it possible to enter into the next. But *between these phases there are situations of crisis*, in which the person concerned seeks for orientation, support and help. These interim situations are open for transcendence, and also for repentance and conversion. Conversion is not infrequently associated with crisis situations of this kind: between youth and early adulthood, in mid-life, in the transition from working life to retirement. The 'immediate' conversion can happen here, but 'continuous' conversion comes about in the modulation of the different phases of life, phases which are reflected in corresponding phases of faith. 'Being a Christian', says Feifel, 'is a formed practice of living.'

Conversion is therefore always a *graduated process*, whether it is a long-term proceeding or a 'sudden', 'momentary' event. Each of the two stretches of the path I have described ('first' and 'second' conversion) can be split up into individual steps. Together these add up to a process with steps that can move forwards or back. In both the Old Testament and the New we find the same structures or phases in this process: a *turning away from the old life*, or the old person ('Adam'), and a *turning to the new life*, or the new person ('Christ'). In every case it is 'the initiative of the God who has always been gracious, fundamentally reconciled and unswervingly faithful' (R. Schulte) that triggers off the process of reflection and new orientation. In the Old Testament this process is an event that is never finished and done with; in the New, conversion stands and falls with the salvation in Christ that is now present. Consequently it is also possible for a person to fall back—or to fall away—into unredeemed existence—hence Leo the Great's admonishment: 'Christian, recognise thy dignity! Thou hast come to partake of the divine nature. Revert not to thine earlier pitiable condition! Live not beneath the dignity that is thine! ... Through the sacrament of baptism thou didst become a temple of the Holy Spirit. Do not through thy sins drive forth the noble Guest who hath taken up his dwelling in thee!' Baptism, that is to say, is no guarantee of grace. The Christian must play his part by working on the *metanoia* event throughout his whole life. Baptism is the beginning and principle of the spiritual struggle; from now on it is a matter of what Origen calls the *exire*, the *relinquere* and the *proficere*—the departing, the leaving behind, and the advancing.

Theologians have continually outlined *stages or phases in the conversion process*. To mention only two of them: Johann Michael Sailer (1751–1832) deduces from the biblical conversion accounts the following four stages: (i) the awakening/softening of the heart; (ii) recognition of the state of sin; (iii) acceptance of this in confession before God and God's representative; (iv) the convert's new life. In our own time, S. McFague has seen the parables as a paradigm for conversion, viewed as the transformation of life evoked by faith. In both the parables and in conversion, our world is split apart, and there is a completely new alignment. This comes about in *three steps*: '*orientation*'—'*disorientation*'—'*reorientation*'. It is in these steps that conversion takes place. Generally and primarily, conversion is not a 'momentary' or sudden experience. Normally speaking it is a painful, life-long process, fraught with doubts, unrest, tensions and ever new ventures.

Schibilsky and Zulehner have studied the theological and pastoral questions that arise here, viewing them in the light of the *sociology of knowledge*. They show how complex and differentiated conversion is 'seen empirically'. For although conversion is a subjective religious experience, thus to a large extent escaping quantification, it is none the less fundamentally open to empirical analysis. The goal of these researches is not to manipulate the process of conversion. The aim is to elucidate its complexity and its inner structure. Biographical interviews suggest that—simplistically presented— conversion has the following stages. Disappointment and surprises break into what has hitherto been a relatively ordered life, lived in a stable system of meaning (religion, denomination). As a result of these disappointments and surprises, questions and probes are put for the first time to the previous system of meaning, and these are also linked with simultaneous, initial contacts with people belonging to a different, new system of meaning. If the person's discontent and disappointment over the first system of meaning are reinforced, not eliminated, he 'emigrates inwardly' or 'outwardly'. The first effect of this emigration is a phase of *reorientation*: contacts to the new group are intensified, comparisons are made between the two systems of meaning, and judgments are formed ('competition'). The result is a kind of 'meaning vacuum': the person begins to experience an orientation crisis, both psychological and physical. This crisis situation is aligned towards decision: the person concerned must either return to the previous system of meaning or he must strike out towards a new one. It is only in the succeeding phase of *consolidation* that conversion also becomes public and avowed. The convert becomes familiar with the new system, the group turns more intensively to its 'new member', and the new member increasingly becomes part of the group, while despising and scorning 'the old one'. At the same time he tries to win support for the new system of meaning among other people, perhaps even among the people whose views he had previously shared.

What is important for pastoral care here is the recognition that conversion is by no means a merely emotional happening. It is *socially constituted and socially anchored*, and has typical features within this sociological framework. The following factors play a decisively important part here: credible people who live out their attitude to things convincingly; people who have a discerning and helpful knowledge of life; a group which conveys the feeling that the new member is accepted and sheltered. For a conversion is only viable and can only remain stable if it issues in permanent communication with the new group. Of course life moves on for the convert. The new identity of faith will have to stand the test in the future too: the temptations of other social and religious attitudes and the challenges of counter-experiences in personal life. Testing and suffering is after all the crucible of faith (see 1 Pet. 1:7). Our own death will become the last, ultimate invitation to conversion—to acceptance of the kingdom of God like a child (see Luke 18.17).

3. MINISTRIES AND HELPS IN CONVERSION

Jesus' invitation to take the path of conversion is an invitation to everyone—to everyone who has been baptised, to Christian groups and congregations, to the Church, and to the whole of humanity. It is intended that the *metanoia* event of Jesus' paschal mystery should make its impact on and in individuals *by way of the Church*—through the proclamation of the Gospel, through the celebration of the liturgy and the sacraments, through unselfish service to the poor and needy, and through the testimony of a redeemed, converted life. This invitation must be given 'for nothing', without compulsion, without threats and without intimidation.

Anyone who sets out on this path of conversion needs *signposts*. These can take the form of companions whom one meets 'by chance', whether personally or in their writings—companions who are officially given as such, or people whom one seeks out and chooses for oneself. The prophets saw themselves as 'aids' to conversion like this. John the Baptist is interpreted by the Christian Church in this sense. Andrew and Philip brought Simon Peter and Nathaniel to meet Jesus. It was when he was on the road that Philip explained the meaning of Scripture to the Ethiopian eunuch, and baptised him. Ananias and Barnabas became for Paul 'the minsters of his conversion', helping him to baptism and acceptance by the congregation in Jerusalem. Through Peter and John, the followers of Jesus in Samaria were incorporated into the one Church, under the leadership of Jerusalem and the company of the twelve. But every minister to conversion acts *in persona Christi*, on Jesus' behalf and in his name. The Emmaus story makes it particularly clear that it is Christ himself who has opened up to us 'the new and living way' (Heb. 10:20). He is the precursor and leader in faith.

The first and most important ministers to conversion, on Christ's behalf, are and remain parents, godparents, members of the house church, and all Christian groups in the congregation who have made it their task to reflect life in the light of the Gospel. All these should in their own way help those who have been baptised to become Christians in the true and conscious sense.

Of growing importance today are the *groups of catechumens*. Children, young people and adults, people who have been baptised and applicants for baptism form a group for a certain limited time, so that they can practise being a Christian together and learn from one another. This is the way the catechumen ought to experience the testimony of faith, for 'becoming a Christian needs examples' (G. Biemer and A. Biesinger). Similar groups of catechumens have also been found helpful for people who are preparing for confirmation and for the sacrament of marriage. New Christian movements, in Germany, for example, the groups of the Neo-Catechumenates, groups for charismatic renewal, the Cursillo movement or the Focolare all try, each in its own way, to guide Christians towards the 'second conversion'. The Taizé community, again, gathers people from different denominations and countries and invites them to join in a 'pilgrimage of reconciliation'. This is seen as a going to meet one another, but also as a new start and a conversion inwardly, towards Christ. The 'Gemeinschaften christlichen Lebens', communities of Christian life, try to let the practice of spiritual exercises lead to the conversion of the whole person, and for this purpose they train 'spiritual sponsors'. All these groups must ask themselves critically (and must allow the same question to be put to them): are they helping to develop personal identity, or are they fastening on people, putting them in bondage and under pressure, like the various sects and new religious groups ('youth religions')? Spiritual leaders especially have to examine themselves, asking: Are we clearing the ground for the *freedom of Christian life*? Or are we producing new dependencies, individually and collectively?

Ministry to conversion by clergy or laity must always be subject to the influence of the Holy Spirit, just as conversion itself is 'the work of the Spirit'. This means that the goal of all spiritual ministry is to help people to find a direct, personal relationship to God—indeed to call into being an experience of God. In contemplating the path of Jesus, mediated to us through Holy Scripture, the person concerned is to become open for the personal God and his tokens of salvation in Jesus Christ. He should develop into 'an identity that has been formed by the Christian faith, an identity that is firmly established and will be viable in a non-Christian environment especially. The convert should find access to a group of Christians and to a Christian congregation' (P. M. Zulehner). Ministry here aims to make possible and encourage personal and existential identity. But the goal is social, ecclesial identity too.

All this applies in a special way to celebration of the sacrament of conversion and reconciliation, which grants the person who has gravely sinned but is repentant the healing encounter with the risen Christ. This sacrament also strengthens and encourages the Christian, with his everyday sins, to remain on the path of consistent, life-long conversion. Here the priest is the officially authorised 'minister of reconciliation', and is equipped with sacramental authority. The *ordo paenitentiae* assumes that the sacrament will be conferred in a spiritual and personal context, far removed from any mechanical, routine or ritualistic practice. Consequently conversation between priest and penitent has become *one* important approach to the ministry of penance: in this dialogue the priest can be experienced as 'minister of the Church' and as 'brother in Christ', helping and counselling, consoling and admonishing, in an existential exposition of the Gospel for the particular situation and in the right of his high office to pronounce absolution in the Church's name. Of course this ministry of the sacrament of penance as counselling, helping and forgiving dialogue requires a particular spiritual and psychological equipment—and hence special training. Moreover, the priest's own attitude, and his readiness for his own conversion, is decisive: am I myself prepared for ever new conversion, and do I allow myself to be accompanied and ministered to in the process?

The *communal service of reconciliation* allows repentant members of the congregation to learn that they stand together before God, in both guilt and reconciliation. These services have an essential importance, moulding the conscience of the individual and making the Church as a whole aware that it is in need of continual renewal and conversion. The German bishops, for example, rightly stress that services of reconciliation should have a firm place in the life of every congregation.

New opportunities for pastoral care and counselling in problematical situations in life (marriage and family, profession, environment, crisis situations) have given priests and laity new functions, some of them shared. Where the sacrament of penance is concerned, these new functions are supportive, but also lighten the load. Anyone who is active in any of these callings of counselling and help needs not only professional competence but spiritual competence too: Christian *diakonia* or ministry is compounded of solidarity and spirituality.

Whatever the place of therapeutic and spiritual counselling as accompaniment to conversion, one thing is clear: conversion has to take place *at the centre of life*—at work, among neighbours, in marriage and family life, in the local congregation, in politics and economic affairs. By turning to one another in our contrition—to the ecumenical community, to the world around, to the community, to life, to responsibility for the world—we are also turning back to God. We must turn away from the powers that bring death and turn to the forces that give life—in us, among us and above us. In this way we shall draw on the advance payment given to us in baptism: 'We have passed out of the zone of death into life' (1 John 3:14).

Translated by Margaret Kohl

Bibliography

S. Barbarić *Umkehr als fundamentale Lehr- und Lernaufgabe christlicher Erwachsenenbildung* (Frankfurt 1985).
K. Baumgartner *Erfahrungen mit dem Bußsakrament*, vols. 1 and 2 (Munich 1978–79).
A. Exeler *Mut zur Umkehr, Einfachheit, Tugend* (Ostfildern 1983); also 'Umkehr—Schritte zur Verwirklichung' *Kat. Blätter* 107 (Munich 1982) 147–161.
S. McFague 'Bekehrung: Leben am Rande des Floßes', *Theologie der Gegenwart* 22 (1979) 1–10.
V. B. Gillespie *Religious Conversion and Personal Identity: How and why people change* (Birmingham, Alabama 1979).
J. Ratzinger 'Metanoia als Grundbefindlichkeit christlicher Existenz' in *Buße und Beichte* ed. E. C. Suttner (Regensburg 1972).
M. Schibilsky *Religiöse Erfahrung und Interaktion* (Stuttgart 1976); also 'Konversion—empirisch gesehen' *Lebendendige Seelsorge* 29 (Würzburg 1978) 165–170.
E. Schillebeeckx *Jesus, an Experiment in Christology* trans. Hubert Hoskins (London 1979).
P. M. Zulehner *Umkehr: Prinzip und Verwirklichung* (Frankfurt 1979).

Michael Sievernich

'Social Sin' and its Acknowledgment

THE THEOLOGY of liberation, which started in Latin America, was inspired by the Gospel's liberating message, and impelled by the social want of the continent's poor. With their talk of 'structural' or 'social' sin, liberation theologians deployed a category[1] which was criticised as fiercely as its soteriological counterpart, 'liberation'; it nevertheless won theological and doctrinal acceptance in the course of elucidation. As a category, it is the outcome of a procedure in which the conventional idea of sin was applied to and 'contextualised' in the existing subcontinental context, but was somewhat transformed in the process, and thus demonstrated yet again the historical malleability of the doctrine of sin.[2] It remains to be seen whether this notion of sin can enrich theological thinking and open up a new epoch of access to the essential Christian expression of penance.

1. BIRTH OF A NEW CATEGORY

A contextual understanding of sin which fits this instance may be deduced from the prophetic struggle of *Bishop Bartolomé de las Casas* in the golden age of New World conquest. He led the fight against avarice (*avaritia*), which had replaced pride (*superbia*) since the convulsions of the high middle ages as the first of the eight capital sins,[3] and that in two senses. On the one hand, in his pastoral capacity as a bishop, he tried to refine the consciences of his fellow countrymen by strictly applying the Church's penitential discipline, and wrote a '*Confesario*'[4] in which he insisted above all on a legally attested duty of restitution of the damage done by plunderers, colonists, slaveowners and arms-dealers. On the other hand, he fought on the legal level against what he saw as the sinfully contrived system of 'ecomienda', still the core of the colonial economy, and pressed the distant Emperor to make structural changes (of a legislative nature). These were enacted, if only for a short time, in the 'Nuevas Leyes' (1542). His struggle concerned sin both in its individual and in its social manifestations. It is not astonishing, therefore, that liberation theologians see Las Casas as their 'Father of the Church', whose decisive inspiration was neither an impulsion to social reform nor mere ethical rebellion, but perception of the presence of Christ in the oppressed indios who were prematurely robbed of their lives by sin.[5]

What Las Casas would seem actually to have anticipated, the liberation theologians would appear to have clarified conceptually in conjunction with the Church's magisterium in regard to the present Latin American social situation. A sketch of the way this has happened can prepare a systematic exposition. The Council should yield a decisive indication in this respect. Vatican II, which introduced the complex of problems relating to sin into its Pastoral Constitution at a relatively late stage, states on the one hand that reason, will, freedom and creativity are maimed by sin,[6] but emphasises, on the other hand, the fact that sin distorts the world and throws history into disarray.[7] Hence pride and egotism 'also put the social environment out of true (ambitum socialem pervertunt)', and 'the objective conditions themselves (ordo rerum) are affected by the results of sin', which in turn offer new occasions of sin.[8] The conciliar texts themselves do not as yet feature the term 'social sin', which nevertheless appears in a early commentary on the Pastoral Constitution.[9]

What the Council left in the air was taken up by theological discourse in Latin America, not to be sure as a topic for academic debate, but on the basis of the complex of acute subcontinental social problems. Here theological reflection was concerned less with conceptual mastery of the problems, but rather, from a spiritually motivated basis, with a practical transformation of the situation. In the first systematic draft of a theology of liberation, Gustavo Gutiérrez defined sin as a social and historical fact. 'Sin is tangible in oppressive structures, in the exploitation of human beings by other human beings, in the domination and enslavement of peoples, races and social classes. Therefore sin appears as fundamental alienation, as the root of a situation of injustice and exploitation'.[10] The theologal aspect which is necessary for every even analogous concept of sin is expressed in the proposition that not only sinful behaviour but its manifestations are an 'affront' to God, inasmuch as they are directed against the order of creation and against humankind made in the divine image. Shortly before his murder in 1980, Archbishop Oscar Romero said when awarded an honorary doctorate in Louvain: 'Above all we are now more aware of what sin is. We know that resistance to God brings about the death of a human being. We know that sin does indeed lead to death. It not only brings about the inward death of the person committing the sin, but produces real, objective death. ... You cannot attack God without attacking people too. The worst assault on God, the worst secularism, consists in turning the children of God, temples of the Holy Spirit, the historical body of Christ, into sacrifices of oppression and injustice, slaves of economic competition, and of chronic political domination.'[11] This and similar statements constantly associated the actual social situation with sin seen as the root of all misery, though without any great interest being shown in the theoretical elucidation of this relationship.

The *Roman Synod of Bishops of 1971* discussed the question of justice in the world. What remained of the synodal document was a torso, but in it the bishops addressed themselves to the newly developing understanding of sin, and talked of 'sin both of individuals and of society as a whole'.[12] Here the *two dimensions were to be found alongside one another for the first time, but without any closer analysis of their relationship*. A critical yet unpolemical document of the International Theological Commission, 'On the Association between Human Welfare and Christian Salvation' (1976), was concerned to elucidate the subject objectively, and considered speaking of 'sinful structures' problematical because talk of sin rightly belonged in the context of a personal decision for freedom. But the document also left no room for doubt 'that the power of sin may allow unrighteous behaviour and injustice entry to socio-economic and political institutions.'[13]

The difficult but successful birth of a *renewed notion of sin oriented to the field of social concerns took place in 1979 in the final Puebla document*. Here the Latin American bishops gave official Church status to a conception emanating from liberation theology. The Puebla document talks occasionally of individual and social sin in the same breath, as it were,[14] yet clearly emphasises social sin, which is understood as the 'objectification of sin in the economic, social, political and ideological-cultural field' (P. 1113). Accordingly, it may be seen as a decisive cause of extreme poverty, from which millions of Latin Americans are compelled to suffer, inasmuch as such poverty is not an accident, 'but the result of economic, social, political and other instances and structures' (P. 28). The document stresses the 'systemic' character which may be assumed by sin, noting that sin also affects entire systems, such as Marxism and liberal capitalism (P. 92), but also stirs up mischief in culture (P. 405). The fact that the category of social sin should never suppress or replace that of individual sin is shown in a mature formulation of the document, which states that, as the divisive force *per se*, sin will always seek to maim the growth of love and community, 'both from the basis of the human heart and from that of the various structures wrought by human beings, in which the sin of those who established those structures has left its destructive mark' (P. 281). Finally, with the apostolic exhortation *Reconciliatio et paenitentia* of John Paul II (1984), *for the first time a document of the magisterium which was binding on the whole Church, began to talk about social sin* and in so doing distinguished three acceptations which feature in the remainder of this article.[15]

2. INDIVIDUAL AND SOCIAL SIN

Christian tradition has always been aware of the fact that *all sins*, however personal they may be, have a *social dimension*; this is apparent in the ecclesial character of penance (*pax cum ecclesia*) or, for instance, in the requirement of restitution for intentional injury. There is just as much biblical testimony (in, for example, the New Testament catalogues of sins), and it is uncontested in tradition, that there are specific sins in the social area which are directly oriented against one's neighbour. There is as little justification for asserting that these sins (such as 'the sins crying out to heaven for justice': the oppression of widows and of the poor, or the refusal of a just wage), which were mentioned in almost all catechisms and handbooks of moral theology, actually affected penitential practice and education, as there is for disputing the widespread fixation on sexual misdemeanours. For centuries a major landowner had more to fear from the Church in sexual than in social matters. Here there is evidence of the still scarcely examined question of the degree of relevance of a situation permeated with sin to moral acknowledgment and standardisation and to an appropriate pastoral policy.[16]

Though Christian tradition has always been aware of this social dimension of sin, but without ever stressing it sufficiently, it is *quite novel to relate talk of sin to social arrangements and structures themselves*: that is, to the social institutions, rules and norms which secure fundamental rights, control the satisfaction of basic needs, and govern interhuman relations. Social formations are neither mere natural instances, nor are they simply the results of an anonymous developmental logic, or of the action of an 'invisible hand' (Adam Smith). In modern times theologal justification and anthropological consensus combine to see them as the results of historical action. If it is true to say that we can no longer argue from the basis of a prestablised natural social order, but understand this order as humanly created, acknowledging that it has to be shaped, then the concomitant reciprocal relationship of individual and society must also raise the question of (moral) behaviour. *Good and sinful behaviour may appear in or be embodied in social arrangements*, which for their own part reciprocally affect individuals, though not determinatively. If this sin embodied in social structures, sin which comes from human beings and reacts on them, is known as 'social sin', we are of course dealing with an analogous concept of sin, for Christian tradition recognises no other kind.

A confrontation with objections which have been raised against talk of social sin, makes their specificity even plainer. *Only individuals and not structures can sin*—such is the objection often made and frequently associated with the fear that ethical quality is to be transferred from the person and located instead in structures, which would be tantamount to a cancellation of freedom and responsibility.[17] It is evident, to be sure, that an institution or structure in itself cannot be the subject of ethical actions, whether good or evil. Structures as such are guiltless. But structures can be objectively evil; as such, according to Clodovis Boff, they are '*pekkaminös*', and for society represent what concupiscence means for the individual: *arising from sin and conducing to sin*. In this sense social structures can become objective manifestations of sin, and actual unfreedom. Those become subjectively guilty who produce or maintain such 'arrangements', make use of them, or are silent accomplices in their persistence.[18] This understanding of the dialectical implications of individual and social sin essentially reflects, in terms of theology of sin, an anthropological datum which is taken as obvious in ecclesiology and in the doctrine of grace: the personal and social structure of human existence.[19] Any theologically aware examination of this relationship which is acquainted with philosophical findings will see talk of social sin as necessary to underpin responsibility for such structures. As against a unilateral 'personalist' schema, according to which individual and society are associated as cause and effect, we are not to prefer a 'socialist' schema, according to which the relationship in question should be reversed in the sense of a primacy of the social. Instead we should argue more for a *reciprocal relationship of equal causation between individual and society*, and respectively between individual and social sin.[20] As the individual by his or her sin co-affects social space, in his or her activity he or she is co-affected by the existing social arrangements. The individual is simultaneously cause and sacrifice of the dominant enmities, conflicts and predicaments (see *Gaudium et spes*, 8). This also illuminates the theme of 'imprisonment' (*cautiverio*) which is often adduced in liberation theology, and which Paul Ricoeur invokes in his analysis of religious profession, and refers to sin. Since imprisonment as a social situation of the people of Israel in Egypt 'became a symbol of sin, this image has revealed the alienating nature of sin. The sinner is "in" a state of sin, just as the Israelites were "in" a state of slavery. Hence sin is an evil in which the human being is involved. Therefore it can be both individual and social at one and the same time.'[21]

3. ACKNOWLEDGMENT OF SOCIAL SIN

If there is such a thing 'as objectified sin, socially established opposition to God',[22] if we may speak in a theologically legitimate and proven way of 'social sin', nevertheless we still have to face the difficult question of its application in specific situations, on the one hand, and of its attachment to individuals on the other hand. Acknowledgment or confession (in the double sense) plays a part in regard to both aspects.

(a) Social Sins and Situations

To be sure, it is not unproblematical to characterise specific social circumstances, political institutions, and legal or economic systems as such, and purely and simply, as social sin. For even apart from their social necessity, none of these extremely complex instances is the exclusive result of sinful activity. Much may be attributed to error and ineptitude; much else to factors and factual determinants outside the remit of moral responsibility. Moreover all these human creations remain subject to a certain degree of imperfection. Therefore a disposition to imperfection is wholly understandable, though of course it should not be invoked as an alibi for the particular factual circumstances, especially not when human dignity is in the balance.

If the category of social sin is not to be reduced to a mere socio-critical token of political morality, and if it is to be of significance beyond the justifiable emphases of prophetic discourse, we have to remember that this explanatory theological category can neither provide (and therefore cannot replace) a social analysis, nor make a reconciliatory theory of justice superfluous, nor yet ignore the autonomy of specialised fields.[23] Given such mediation, in certain situations (such as persistent domination by force, or radical injustice, a public order which negates human rights or a legal system which suppresses human dignity), it is not only possible but requisite *to characterise as sinful this transformation of social arrangements into their opposites.*

Friedrich Spee demonstrated in an exemplary manner how that can happen; he contested the collective witch hunts of his century from his experience as confessor of the accused. By means of skilful legal arguments he exposed the witch trials as the instrument producing the very same sinful situation which one wished to remove. In his anonymously published manifesto *Cautio criminalis*[24] he also ascribed the responsibility for this mortal fanaticism to specific groups of people, and named the princes and their advisers, divines, legal experts and the people. Spee saw his behaviour as a matter of conscience, which bound him to acknowledge the truth before the thrones of princes and bishops. Today, too, a situation marked by sin can make a choice necessary, such as the 'predominant option for the poor' of the Latin American Church, which enjoys '*status confessionis*' in that social situation.

(b) Social Sin and Persons

In the ascription of social sin to individuals or to groups of individuals, three modes of question are to be distinguished: in regard to the *past*, the question of (guilty) *participation*; in regard to the *present*, the question of the mode and method of *avowal*; and in regard to the *future*, the question finally of a *new mode of practice*.

(i) Participation

Since social sin is always in a dialectical relation with the sinful behaviour of individuals in history and in the present, we experience the resultant complex of problems relating to guilty, or even merely factual participation in that behaviour, as well as responsibility for those social orders in which the sin is expressed and hides. Who is guilty of racist prejudice or of the brutal domination of the 'Third Reich' in Germany, of the arms race, of the increasing impoverishment of the so-called 'Third World', of ideologies replete with hatred, or of asymmetrical trade relations? Clearly we should beware of wholesale ascriptions of guilt, as of cheap accusations of scapegoats. In the individual case, it is impossible to distribute guilt as originally incurred by individuals or groups. That does not mean, however, that all individuals can go scotfree of guilt. Even if the sinful social formations are difficult to isolate, that does not justify leaving them to themselves and suspending one's own responsibility for them. Consequently, but without preaching collective guilt, a *threefold ascription of social* sin to individuals may be outlined. First there is coresponsibility in the sense of a *nolens volens* given solidarity of implication in the particular situation in which the individual or a nation consciously bears the sinful burden of history. Then there is coresponsibility in the sense of acknowledgment of, and accountability for, an objectively wrong even if not subjectively evil action.[25] Third and last, there is joint guilt in the sense of effective participation by deed or omission, the extent of the personal involvement in which is of course no longer to be defined. The decisive factor in all three modes of ascription remains the fact that it cannot be imputed from without, but can only be acknowledged by the individual according to best knowledge and conscience. External impulses such as a moral appeal or prophetic discourse can of course promote this 'process of subjectification', but may also delay it.

This kind of *conscious assumption* also implies the recognition that the evil which is attributable to human action in freedom cannot be rationalised and 'justly' apportioned or written off by the individual. Social sin belongs to the '*mysterium inquitatis*' (2 Thess 2:7), which cries out for redemption by God as the Lord of history, and reveals the need for redemption, the recognition of which could go beyond the acknowledgment of participative implication in social sin. Social sin as collective implication, as 'imprisonment' in sin, indicates that 'the basic problematics of existence is less that of freedom in the sense of a choice to be made in the face of a radical alternative, and much more that of liberation. The person imprisoned in sin is one who has to be liberated. All our ideas of salvation, redemption—that is, of ransom—proceed from this first token.'[26]

(ii) *Acknowledgment*

The acknowledgment of factual, objective or subjective participation in social sin is to be seen as the beginning of a conversion and leads to recognition, to confession before God (*coram Deo*), as the sole locus of any hope of liberating redemption. Since confession of the most individual sins does not remain a private matter, in so far as it takes place in the Church as the location of social grace, the question occurs of how acknowledgment of social sin is *also to be made before others* (*coram hominibus*). The decisive location of such an ecclesially public acknowledgment of implication is the common confession of several individuals; or the public confession of several individuals; or the public confession of groups, nations and institutions. '*Confessio peccatorum*' may also be understood literally as 'a harmonised open acknowledgment by sinners of their guilt'. Because guilt is acknowledged in the community, and in common, this very confession establishes a new community.[27]

This aspect of *confession in common* is formative of community and supports reconciliation; it becomes actual when, for example, the bishops of Peru write (as in 1969): 'We acknowledge that we as Christians through inadequate loyalty to the Gospel have contributed to the present situation of injustice with our words, attitudes, omissions and silence'.[28] Or when the Evangelical Church in Germany in its 'Stuttgart Declaration' of 1945 spoke of a 'solidarity of guilt' and acknowledged: 'Through us infinite suffering has been extended to many peoples and countries ... To be sure, for many long years in the name of Jesus Christ we combated the spirit which found hideous expression in the Nazi rule of violence; but we accuse ourselves of not having professed more courageously, not having prayed more loyally, not having believed more joyously, and not having loved more powerfully.'[29] But outside the Church too, in the political sphere, such acknowledgments are requisite, where they keep alive a painful memory and assume the responsibility of the burdens of history.[30] Without such confessions it would be difficult to reach any reconciliation and understanding between groups, classes and nations.

Precisely the Church of Jesus Christ is required to provide room for circumscribed confession as a sign of the 'duty of reconciliation' (2 Cor. 5:18) with which it is charged. The rich variety of ecclesial penitential traditions is as much an encouragement to this as the essentially theological structure of penance. The '*Ordo paenitentiae*' (1973), the order of penance of the Catholic Church, opens up the liturgical context of communal celebration of reconciliation (with a confession and absolution of the individual, and with a general confession and general absolution) as well as penitential services, in which forms of confession appropriate to social sin have or, better, could have a place—for practice, in Europe at least, seems a long way from that. Moreover the tendency of pastoral strategy is not to favour communual forms of penance as against individual confession, when the former might well help to make the latter more popular. Apart from the liturgically available forms of penance there is of course a wide range of other possibilities. The category of social sin, for instance, could enable us to understand more comprehensively than hitherto the classical trinity of penitential fasting, prayer and alms (see Matt. 6:1–10).

Whatever form the common acknowledgment of implication in sin may take, the '*mea culpa*' will always have to be associated with 'forgive us our trespasses'. The acknowledgment of sins (*confessio peccatorum*) must be marked by a simultaneous offering of a confession of praise (*confessio laudis*) to God.

(iii) *Conversion*

Confession would remain incomplete if it did not correspond to a *new turning to God* corresponding to the rejection of sin. This movement is expressed in terms of one's recourse to one's neighbour. For both modes of conversion, in the sense of the dual commandment of love (Matt. 22:36–38), are not ranged incommunicably alongside one another, but are indissolubly linked one with the other. Just as conversion to God necessarily involves recourse to the other as one's brother, and would be incomplete without that (see 1 John 4:20), conversely conversion to the least becomes the way in which the relationship with Christ is mediated (see Matt. 25:40). If this was always at least theoretically clear in Christian tradition, nowadays we must also remember that conversion to one's neighbour does not stop at intersubjective and charitable instances, but *includes institutionally mediated relationships*. Therefore the theology of liberation firmly emphasises the fact that *conversion of the heart and improvement of structures are not alternatives but must go hand in hand*. 'Christians who are conscious of the association between the personal and structural can no longer remain satisfied with personal sanctity and the conversion of the heart alone. They know that (to be personally graced) they must struggle to ensure that social structures are changed from the roots up. Being converted means opening oneself up.'[31] In order to sail unscathed between the Scylla of pure inward conversion and the Charybdis of purely external change, one has to *change oneself and circumstances simultaneously*. The Puebla document stresses the fact that 'the transformation of structures is an external expression of inward conversion' (P. 1221) and claims that the reality of the Latin American situation demands a personal conversion and really profound structural alterations which do justice to popular efforts for social justice (cf. P. 30). If in this perspective of practical conversion before all else, its active dimensions were transferred to the macrosocial realm of struggle against social sin, then the *passion dimension* also has to be stressed, because of the human inability to prevent or to overcome evil and suffering in history, which appears no less enjoined '*ad agonem*' (see DS 1515). Here too we must recall the 'pathic constitution' of Christian practice (J. B. Metz). 'Today broad sections of humanity are called to suffer and accept in a penitential mood evil structures of an economic, social or political nature. For many, the attempt to withdraw from cooperation with such structures implies a sensitive indifference to goods and position, which can also be a form of enjoined penance. Furthermore, the attempt to make tolerable or to remove evil structures can lead to heavy burdens (even to that of persecution) which have to be borne in the spirit of penance'.[32] A new practice of faithful conversion understood thus cannot be dismissed as 'obedient responsibility' before the given arrangements and norms, but must undertake normative formal responsibility for them, even if *prima facie* the complexity of social formations makes it difficult to recognise any points of attack.[33] This responsibility, which has to be borne 'by merciful scepticism' (H. Jonas) in regard to the utopian possibilities of mankind, is only protected from too great a demand by its gift of divine liberation from sin and death, and therefore realises that it is duty-bound to forgiveness.[34]

Only the freedom liberated by Christ's cross and resurrection (Gal. 5:1) can suppress social sin as actual unfreedom, without bringing the enemy forth again.

Translated by J. G. Cumming

Notes

1. See extensively in M. Sievernich *Schuld und Sünder in der Theologie der Gegenwart* (Frankfurt 1983) pp. 232–282.

2. See M. Sievernich 'Plasticidad de la doctrina del pecado e inculturación del Evangelio' in Stromata 41 (1985) 407–417.

3. See L. K. Little 'Pride goes before avarice. Social change and the vices in Latin Christendom' in American Historical Review 76 (1971) 16–49.

4. See A. Gutiérrez 'El "confesionario" de Bartolomé de las Casas' in Ciencia Tomista 102 (1975) 249–278.

5. On this fundamental christological intuition see Ph.-I. André-Vincent Bartolomé de las Casas. Prophète du Nouveau Monde (Paris 1980).

6. Pastoral Constitution Gaudium et spes Nos. 15, 78, 17, 37.

7. Ibid., No. 39, 40.

8. Ibid., No. 25.

9. W. Weber and A. Rauschek 'Die menschliche Gemeinschaft' in Die Kirche in der Welt von Heute, Untersuchungen und Kommentare zur Pastoralkonstitution 'Gaudium et Spes' des II. Vatikanischen Konzils ed. G. Barauna (Salzberg 1967) p. 184.

10. G. Gutiérrez Teologia de la liberación (Salamanca 1972) p. 237.

11. O. Romero Die politische Dimension des Glaubens. Basis, Gemeinde und Befreiung ed. A. Reiser and P. G. Schoenborn (Wuppertal 1981) p. 160.

12. De iustitia in mundo No. 52: Acta Apostolicae Sedis 63 (1971) p. 935.

13. The document is to be found in K. Lehmann Theologie der Befreiung (Einsiedeln 1977) pp. 173–195, here p. 187.

14. III Conferencia General del Episcopado Latinoamericano. Puebla, La Evangelizacón en el presente y en el gujtoro de América Latina (Bogotà 1979); hereinafter referred to as 'P', here P. 73, 487, 1258.)

15. 'Reconciliatio et paenitentia' No. 16: Acta Apostolicae Sedis 77 (1985) pp. 213–17.

16. See in this respect J. Fuchs 'The Sin of the World and Normative Morality' in Gregorianum 61 (1980) 51–76.

17. See J. Ratzinger 'Der Mut zur Unvollkommenheit und zum Ethos' in Frankfurter Allgemeine Zeitung No. 171 (Frankfurt 1984), and also the instruction of the Congregation for the Doctrine of Faith 'Libertatus nuntius' No. IV, 14 and 15 Acta Apostolicae Sedis 76 (1984) p. 885.

18. See C. Boff—A. Libànio Pecado social y conversion estructural (Bogota 1978).

19. See the model at P. Fransen 'Das neue Sein des Menschen in Christus' Mysterium Salutis IV/ii (Einsiedeln 1973) pp. 939–951.

20. See M. Kehl 'Option fur die Armen. Marxistische Gesellschaftsanalyse und katholische Dogmatick' ed. W. Loser, K. Lehmann and M. Lutz-Bachmann, in Dogmen-Geschichte und katholische Theologie (Wurzburg 1985) pp. 492–496.

21. P. Ricoeur Finitude et culpabilité, II: La Symbolique du Mal (Paris 1960).

22. P. Hünermann, 'Evangelium der Freiheit', in Gott im Aufbruch, ed. P. Hünermann and G.-D. Fischer (Freiburg 1974).

23. On the question of mediation, see C. Boff Teologia e Práctica. Teologia do Politico et suas medições (Petropolis 1978).

24. Cautio criminalis seu de processibus contra sagas liber (Rinteln 1631); see H. Zwetsloot Friedrich Spee und die Hexenprozesse (Trier 1954).

25. Here, for example, we are concerned with coresponsibility in the international armaments race, which represents objectively a misappropriation of vast sums, in so far as the expensive process of arms manufacture contradicts the unsatisfied basic needs of existence in the poor countries. Since the Council (*Gaudium et spes* No. 81) this relationship has been the persistent teaching of the popes.

26. P. Ricoeur, the work cited in note 21, p. 110.

27. P. Henrici '... wie auch wir vergeben unsern Schuldigern': Philosophische Überlegungen zum Busssakrament' in *Communio* 13 (1984) 389–405, here 398.

28. Quoted in Gutiérrez, the work cited in note 10, p. 102.

29. For a discussion of this explanation see G. Bessier-G. Sauter *Wie Christen ihre Schuld bekennen* (Göttingen 1985); M. Honecker 'Geschichtliche Schuld und kirchliches Bekenntnis' in *Theologische Zeitschrift* 42 (1986) 132–158.

30. As paradigmatic in this sense I would cite the political address of the Federal German President given on the 40th anniversary of the German capitulation: R. von Weizsäcker *Von Deutschland aus* (Berlin 1985) pp. 11–35.

31. L. Boff *A graça libertadora no mundo* (Petropolis 1977).

32. 'Internationale Theologenkommission, über Versöhnung und Busse' *Communio* 13 (1984) 44–46.

33. This helpful distinction is taken from W. Korff *Norm und Sittlichkeit. Untersuchungen zu Logik der normativen Vernunft* (Mainz 1973) p. 73.

34. See J. Sobrino 'Latin America: Place of Sin and Place of Forgiveness', in *Concilium* 184 (1986) pp. 45–86.

Norbert Mette

Children's Confession—a Plea for a Child-centred Practice of Penance and Reconciliation

'AT AN early age—I was scarcely eight years old—I had to go to confession. Just think of it: a child of eight, knowing nothing of good and evil, was supposed to know when and how often it had "sinned". A special prayer-room was prepared in the institution so that we could be assembled for prayer at any time. And the very next thing we were told was, "That is a sin, and now your guardian angel is crying because of you". I cannot forget the way we were threatened and terrified with the "evil spirit", the devil and hell.'[1] There is nothing exceptional about these memories of someone who felt tormented by the practice of confession as a child growing up in a Catholic orphanage. A great amount of damage has been done to individuals as a result of an *anxiety-ridden practice of confession from early childhood*, matched by references to guilt and sin in preaching and catechesis. This is doubtless one of the factors leading to the present crisis in the traditional practice of penance. Many people have felt a profound sense of liberation in having finally emancipated themselves from it and from its associated anxieties and scruples.

As far as we can see, today's children are generally no longer crippled by such experiences as a result of their introduction to confession. In catechesis the God who forgives has largely replaced the God who punishes or at least moved him into the background. Furthermore—and this is something that children are quick to notice—many parents regard first confession (like first communion) simply as part and parcel of the growing-up process in the context of popular church customs, albeit without it having any further impact on life.

64

This situation, i.e., that children are to be introduced to the practice of individual confession at a time when the adult parishioners are hardly having recourse to it any more, causes pastoral workers and concerned parents to ask 'whether what we are doing with the children is pastorally meaningful and honest'.[2] One thing is certain: the problem is too pressing for us to simply accept the fact that recently all discussion of it was 'officially and resolutely flattened'—in the words of A. Exeler.[3]

1. OFFICIAL CHURCH REGULATIONS CONCERNING THE TIME FOR FIRST CONFESSION

Can. 914 CIC (1983) presupposes that *children's first communion should be preceded by 'prior sacramental confession'*, and Can. 989 goes on to lay down the 'reaching of the age of discretion' as the time when confession becomes an obligation. Thus the new canon law has adopted the March 1977 decision of both the Congregations for the Liturgy and that for the Clergy, namely, that in general it is (no longer) permissible to celebrate first communion before the reception of the sacrament of penance.[4] In the very same year the German bishops conference issued a revised version of its 1973 guidelines on the time for first confession, which had asserted that while as a rule children should be brought to first confession before first communion, exceptions were to be provided for 'at the explicit request of the parents';[5] now the revised version makes no mention of possible exceptions. Local pastors are to be responsible for observing the sequence first confession—first communion; the parents' role is to 'share' in this responsibility.[6]

This meant that, as far as the territory governed by the German bishops' conference was concerned (and in contrast to other local churches, which managed without clear guidelines), a definite line had been drawn *bringing to an end an 'experimental period'* of at the most ten years. During these ten years experience had been gathered with regard to introducing children to the sacrement of penance in a way appropriate to them. Observations from pastors and those involved in religious education concerning the customary catechesis and practice of children's confession had been included for the first time in the 'Outline of Religious Instruction' issued in 1967 by the German bishops: the 4th school year was recommended as the time for children to be introduced to the sacrament of penance, whereas the 2nd school year was proposed as the time for first communion.[7]

This recommendation was doubtless supported by the 1964 'Guidelines for Children's Confession and Children's Communion' issued for his diocese by Bishop Moors of Roermond (Netherlands), which envisaged a graded introduction of children to penance according to their state of maturity. These

'Guidelines' met with considerable acclaim in the German-speaking debate on religious education.[8]

A similar practice began to establish itself in many US dioceses. At the 1971 International Catechetical Congress in Rome there were reports from different parts of the worldwide Church on the positive results experienced from the *new sequence: First communion—first confession.*

It must have seemed all the more baffling, therefore, to find that the *General Catechetical Directory*, published in the same year, contained an Addendum which harked back to the Decree 'Quam Singulari' of Pius X (1910), once more insisting on the other, traditional sequence and substantiating it with anthropological and theological references.[9] True, Cardinal Wright, Prefect of the Congregation for the Clergy, pointed out that this text had no power in law; but two years later the Congregations for the Liturgy and the Clergy turned down an express wish addressed to the Holy See by the bishops' conference of the USA, declaring—in 'Sanctus Pontifex', and once again referring to 'Quam Singulari'—that all experiments in this area were to be brought to an end.[10]

As a result of this, the relevant section in the final document issued at the 1974 General Synod of the Dioceses in the Federal Republic of Germany entitled 'Central pastoral issues in contemporary sacramental practice' has no greater status, in point of fact, than that of a non-binding expression of opinion. It says: 'In our social situation the time for the first reception of the sacrament of penance—and the same applies to the first reception of the Eucharist—can no longer be tied automatically to the child's age or school year. What is decisive is the actual faith-situation of the child and, above all, its family. These fundamental considerations show that the crucial question is not whether the child should receive the sacrament of penance before or after the first communion.' In any case the wishes of the parents are to be given due weight.[11]

2. THE DEBATE OF THE SEQUENCE FIRST CONFESSION—FIRST COMMUNION

In the Vatican documents referred to the following reasons are adduced in favour of the sequence First confession—first communion: from the 'age of reason or of discretion' children (like adult believers) have a right to receive the sacrament of penance, the sacrament of reconciliation. In estimating when this age of reason is attained ('Quam Singulari' speaks of 'the time around the seventh year of life'—DS 3530), psychological research is regarded as helpful, yet to depend upon it entirely would be to encourage a fateful 'psychologism' which would not do justice to the theological character of this sacrament.—

Even if, according to received Church teaching, children were not as a rule obliged to make their confession, it is asserted that they benefit from an early familiarity with the sacrament of penance: it *deepens their confidence in God's love and mercy* and heightens their sensitivity to sin and their sense of penitence.

Though children must not be given the impression that confession is necessary before receiving the Eucharist, it is maintained that confession 'increases the child's good dispositions for receiving the Eucharist'.[12] Reference is made to the Pauline exhortation of 1 Cor. 11:28, which also applies to children; this strongly indicates the need for the help of a confessor.

It is expected that if children are properly instructed concerning the sacrament of penance they will value it all their life long and reach an even deeper understanding of it in accordance with their personal development.— It is affirmed, moreover, that the sequence First confession—first communion has proved its worth down the centuries, and was as such promulgated authoritatively by Pius X in the general Decree.

Those who advocate a different and at least more open ruling point out that this latter argument, in particular, will not hold water.

In the first place—and this applies to the Church's penitential practice as a whole—it is impossible to establish *historical continuity* with regard to children's confession, the origins of which (in contrast to chilren's communion) are hidden in obscurity. Even if the IV. Lateran Council (see DS 812) set the 'age of discretion' as the criterion for a regular participation in the sacraments of Eucharist and penance, both theological interpretation and pastoral practice have taken highly diverse forms right down to the present century.[13]

Secondly, so the objection runs, it is erroneous to take the general Decree of Pius X as a decision regarding the age of first confession since its concerns were of a different kind (namely, early and frequent reception of communion and the countering of abuses in this area).[14]

In addition the received sequence of sacraments is challenged by the following objections arising from theology, pastoral practice and the teaching of religion: —Children below the age of 8–9 are not yet capable of understanding the real meaning of guilt and sin. Consequently they are not capable of committing grave sin. While it is relatively easy to acquaint them with the 'technique of confession' and give them an 'experience of achievement' that goes with it, it is difficult to inculcate that wider understanding of the sacrament of penance as a concrete form of Christian penance and conversion which Vatican II, in particular, once more brought into prominence. Introducing them to confession too early brings the danger 'that, as regards the education of conscience and the practice of confession, young people and adults will remain fixed at the level of what they learned in childhood'.[15]

It has been observed time and again that, in the case of the sequence First confession—first communion, the *eucharistic catechesis is given less thorough treatment* because catechesis on confession takes up the major part of the time available. Quite apart from this the children easily get the fixed idea that they have to produce 'achievement' of one kind or another in order to be worthy of receiving the Eucharist. This means that there is the danger of exaggerated fears or self-righteousness staying with them for life.

As we have already indicated, a further objection arises out of the *changed pattern of confession among adults*. For 'we can only successfully introduce children to confession if it is something practised by adults. The widely-observed fact that children give up confession at the latest after being confirmed is not as a rule due to faulty preparation but to the fact that the tradition is no longer alive in the parish community. So we must seriously ask ourselves whether we ought to introduce children to the sacrament of penance at all. For the present situation also teaches them that it is something for children (since adults no longer do it). When I grow up I'll not need it any more. Are we not—unintentionally—endangering the seriousness of the sacrament of penance and *branding it as a sacrament for children*? Are we not in fact leading the children away from the sacrament instead of towards it?'[16] People sometimes try to attribute the changed habits to the 'experimentation' of recent years, but clearly this does not follow.

One is left with the suspicion that the official Church's rigidity with regard to an early age for first confession is traceable, in part, to the same pastoral principle that governed the decision of the IV. Lateran Council: namely, the necessity of gaining a hold over the faithful.[17]

Despite differences of opinion a broad consensus has emerged with regard to at least two points:

a) It is insufficient to provide a single introduction to the sacrament of penance; it needs ongoing development and deepening.

b) Such development and deepening is the responsibilty of the whole parish community; hence parents should be involved in catechesis for confession as far as possible.

3. CHILDREN AND ADULTS ON THE WAY TOWARDS A 'CULTURE OF RECONCILIATION'

The arguments for and against show that the *issue of the age for first confession and children's confession in general requires further clarification*.

Official Church pronouncements and canon law regulations cannot simply declare the matter solved. There are indications that theologically responsible and pastorally feasible solutions can only be developed if the problems are situated in a larger context. The concluding document of the synod to which we have referred rightly insists that 'the education of children for penance' must be seen and grasped 'as an ever-present task of Christian education',[18] i.e., it must be connected with growth in faith and participation in the life of the community.

In such a context the traditional catechesis for penance, and the practice of children's confession for which it calls, shows instances of grave neglect and error, ranging from the problematical equating of penance and confession to the over-emphasis on guilt and sin and the sublime misuse of confession as a means of education. This often led to the faulty attitudes which A. Gorres termed 'Catholicist', namely, legalistic moralism and rigorism, compulsive scrupulosity, deference to authority, the loss of spontaneity, and others, connected with an anxiety-ridden religious and Church practice which, furthermore, was strongly individualist and sacramentalist.[19] Or, on the other hand, people acquired 'techniques' of 'mitigating' the burdens of confession: by objectifying the understanding of sin it was possible to go through the practice of confession (which in any case could be repeated at any time) without it having any more profound effect on one's way of life.[20]

These things must be kept in mind lest we make the mistake of evaluating the changes in the pattern of confession exclusively negatively. True—in terms of our topic—they have put a question mark over the traditional way of bringing children to the sacrament of penance. But this simply lays on us the wholesome obligation to devote *more attention to the child and its specific life-situation.* In fact, if we look at the available catechetical material,[21] it seems it has become accepted by now that children must be introduced to penance in a way that corresponds to their development as children, that it must link up with children's diverse worlds of experience, and that parents must be involved in this training as far as possible—indeed, they should initiate it. Nor are the 'official' forms of the sacrament of penance the only goal of penitential education; attempts are being made to acquaint children with the manifold forms of the forgiveness of sins and reconciliation; various modes of liturgical celebration are being kept open.

However, if such approaches are not to remain simply 'loopholes' in the prescribed regulations, they must be accompanied by deeper reflection on the fundamental question, i.e., what, in fact, is the *status of the experience of guilt and sin,* and of the practice of forgiveness and reconciliation with children at the present time, and what this means for penitential education. While the dominant view was that the child was fundamentally bad and involuntarily tended to evil—which meant that everything had to be done to break its will as soon as possible—an early penitential education and practice seemed essential for the child's salvation. Where this anthropological and theological background is no longer there, such education and practice run the danger of being simply a helpful and yet basically dispensable element of moral education, governed by the modern, middle-class understanding of religion as a moral institution (for children).

In the context of present-day views of education, talk of sin before God and the forgiveness of sin by God, if it is unconnected with moral training and development, is repellent. It is suspected—and not without reason, if we recall the way it has been misused—of obstructing the young person's striving for autonomy by imprisoning him in heteronomy. On the other hand the sphere of education also manifests the effects of that 'hidden illusion of innocence which permeates our society and enables us to find guilt and failure (if at all) only in "the others" '.[22] How are children to become aware of their own culpability and learn to cope with it if their life with adults familiarises them with methods of 'excusing' themselves for everything?

This context yields *two basic presuppositions* which should be regarded as outline conditions for an adequate solution of the problems of 'children's confession':

a) If it is to do justice to the child, the practice of penance and reconciliation must be experienced as part of a more comprehensive *'culture of forgiveness and reconciliation'*.

b) If children are to be introduced and initiated into the practice of penance and the sacrament of penance, they must be taken seriously as acting subjects of their own actions; penitential education must follow their own ego-development and *adapt itself to their psychic dispositions*.

In concrete terms this means that we must not become fixated on individual confession as an optimum form of the forgiveness of sins which must be aimed for from early years (although its presupposes the ability to say 'I' in a thoroughly personal and unconfused way). To do this would be to block the path to that *broad spectrum of ways and forms of forgiveness and reconciliation which manifest the wealth of the divine mercy*, or at least cause them to be undervalued. There is much evidence to show that it is much easier to elicit an appreciation for sacramental and ritual forms if children have carefully been led to discover the manifold ways in which sins are forgiven and have acquired experience of this. At this age what is needed and what must be promoted is a practice of penance that no longer cultivates guilt feelings but corresponds to the particular stage of culpability and helps the child to mature in its awareness of its own guilt.[23]

The received sacramental symbolism of *penal judgment* leads to more problems, seen in the context of child development. It hardly corresponds to the Gospel either, which speaks of a turning-away from the accustomed—punitive and didactic—approach to children: it is children who are put forward as examples of that 'conversion learning process' (J. Werbick) which comes about through the experience of God's unconditional love (see Mark 10:13–16 parr). This is not to invoke a supposed 'innocence' on the part of children. On the contrary, learning how to be an 'I', to identify and distinguish one's own claims and needs from those of others, is not a straight path but a process fraught with crises. On the one hand, children must develop and try out their own will in order to attain self-dependence; they must 'affirm' themselves vis-a-vis others, most importantly their own parents, and demonstrate their powers of achievement. On the other hand, without consciously intending it, their own 'self-will' is bound to hurt others and dominate them; they are bound to try to gain recognition at the cost of others.[24] It is not right to speak of sin here. Yet children can find it liberating to experience these ambivalences and be able to make up for things they have done wrong, to realise that they do not have to be fixated on things done in the past but can begin again. In embryo, in fact, this embodies the anthropological content of the individual elements of the sacrament of penance.

We know that in their dealings with one another and with adults children have an astonishing imagination and creativity (provided they are not inhibited) in expressing themselves in fundamental gestures of forgiveness and 'starting again'; why should not their behaviour provide stimuli for the liturgical celebration of this event? What is necessary for the building-up of a 'culture of reconciliation' beginning with everyday things is an atmosphere of unreserved acceptance; creating and maintaining it can make tremendous demands of the adults involved as well since they have to bring a great deal to the encounter. It is not easy for the adult not to repress these experiences of failure but to admit them and where appropriate 'to be ready to be corrected and changed by the child's questionings'.[25] But it can be an experience of great significance for life if the child sees that adults are not always the stronger and superior ones and that they too can ask to be forgiven. To that extent Christian education may be seen as finding its theologically most appropriate and pedagogically most honest expression 'when parents and children, teachers and pupils, adults and young people are able to join together in confessing their sins',[26] allowing God to enable them to learn from failure and to build a world together.

If penance is practised at this fundamental level by children and adults as a constant process of cultivating a 'culture of reconciliation', the Christian community is obliged to examine the given socialisation conditions to see how far they are helpful or a hindrance. Where necessary it must draw attention in particular to the right of children to a space appropriate to them (and this applies to the Church too), protesting against that social sin which cites the 'practical constraints' of an increasingly more complex society as an excuse for limiting or preventing children from being children and having a childhood.[27]

Translated by Graham Harrison

Notes

1. H. G. Dikreiter *Vom Waisenhaus zur Fabrik* (1914), quoted in L. Fertig *Zeitgeist und Erziehungskunst* (Darmstadt 1984) p. 107.

2. R. Waltermann 'Ist Beichten Kindersache?' in *KatBl* 3 (1986) 309.—The following observations are primarly concerned with the German-speaking region.

3. A. Exeler 'Einige Hinweise auf die gegenwärtige religionspädagogische Landschaft' in *KatBl* 105 (1980) 124–129(126).

4. See *Kirchliches Amtsblatt der Diözese Münster* 1977, art. 236.

5. *Ibid.* 1973, art. 289.

6. *Ibid.* 1978, art. 15.

7. See *Rahmenplan fur die Glaubensunterweisung* (Munich 1967) p. 39.

8. See *Altersgemässe Kinderbeicht* ed. F. Heggen (Freiburg 1966).

9. See *General Catechetical Directory* (C. T. S. London 1973) pp. 100–104.

10. See AAS 65 (1973) p. 411.

11. *Gemeinsame Synode der Bistümer in der Bundesrepublik Deutschland.* ed. L. Bertsch et al. (Freiburg 1976) I pp. 238–275 (274); *ibid.* pp. 266ff.—For more detail on this section, see B. A. Haggerty 'Studiendokument zur Praxis von Erstkommunion und Erstbeichte' in *KatBl* 99 (1974) 257–280; T. F. Sullivan 'The Directory and First Confession' in *The Living Light* (1979) 192–208.

12. *General Catechetical Directory,* cited in note 9, p. 103.

13. See B. A. Haggerty, the article cited in note 11, esp. 258–270.

14. See B. A. Haggerty, the article cited in note 11, 265–269; T. F. Sullivan, the article cited in note 11, 200ff.; M. F. X. Janssen 'Beichte vor der Erstkommunion' in *Diakonia* 5 (1974) 117–123.

15. A. Zenner in *KatBl* 99 (1974) 343.

16. B. Ort 'Das Sakrament der Busse im Religionsunterricht' in W. Albrecht et al. *Zur Grundlegung des Sakramentenunterrichts* (Donauwörth 1983) pp. 74–87(77).

17. See I. W. Frank 'Beichte. II. Mittelalter' in *TRE V*, 414–421 esp. 417ff.

18. See 'Schwerpunkte heutiger Sakramentenpastoral', in the volume cited in note 11, p. 267.

19. See A. Görres 'Pathologie des katholischen Christentums' in *HPTh* II/1, 277–343.

20. See H. Geller 'Einstellungen zur Beichte' in *Ökumenische Praxis* ed. P. Lengsfeld (Stuttgart 1984) esp. pp. 367ff.

21. See K. Baumgartner 'Materialien zur Buss- und Beichterziehung von Kindern und Jugendlichen' in *KatBl* 106 (1981) 578–581.

22. Concluding Synod Document: 'Unsere Hoffnung' in the work edited by L. Bertsch et al., cited in note 11, pp. 84–111(93).

23. 'As long as we are developing, each confession is our first.' Thus F. Oser 'Wann ist Erstbeichte?' in *Das Gewissen im pädagogischen Feld* ed. F. Oser (Olten 1973) pp. 101–130(115).

24. A development of penitential theology corresponding to personal development is to be found in J. Werbick *Glaube im Kontext* (Einsiedeln 1983), esp. pp. 217ff.

25. E. Peukert 'Wie und woraufhin soll erzogen werden' in *Welt des Kindes* 64 (1986) 105–110(109).

26. E. E. Nipkow *Grundfragen der Religionspädagogik* (Gütersloh 1982) iv p. 43.

27. See the impressive section 51f. in 'De iustitia in mundo'.

Kabasele-Lumbala

Sin, confession and reconciliation in Africa

Introduction

OVER THE past twelve years the word inculturation has entered theological language in Africa. It has been and is used to indicate the current perspective of theological investigation among the new peoples in the Church. This perspective consists of *making the message of Christ and the Christian experience of the West incarnate in the centuries-old and living traditions of Black Africa.* More and more I am convinced that *rites and celebrations* are the most auspicious contexts for this exchange to take shape and to show us in its living reality a Word that becomes flesh. This fits in moreover with the nature of rites as ways of answering the real questions arising from experience that man asks himself, questions that concern who and what he is and the world in which he lives.

Rites of reconciliation form part of the fundamental rites of Black African societies: they provide both nourishment and cure, they create harmony within society, they mend and re-establish the balance that has been broken. That is why they appear at the most important and most crucial moments in people's lives: they are thus closely tied to a particular understanding of the world and of man, to a particular individual and social ethic. Christian rites of reconciliation convey analogous elements which, however, are not necessarily congruent with those expressed by the traditional rites of reconciliation of Black Africa. Hence the need for detailed mediation: the aim of this essay is to introduce us to where this is taking place.

In writing this I have benefited from the diversity of origin of the students at the theological faculty of Kinshasa. This complemented and broadened what I had learned as pastor of a community. What these students had to say about their experiences in their communities was an invaluable source for me. In 1974 the same faculty held a theological conference devoted to the subject we are concerned with.[1] From the evidence of a host of delegates from different African countries we have been able to extract *certain constants* bearing on this question: the fundamental aim of these rites of reconciliation, the understanding of man that underlies them, and the corresponding understanding of wrong-doing and ethics. We shall depend on these constants for a rapid investigation of the partial attempts at synthesis between the old and the new.

To begin with we shall confine ourselves to some observations on the *crisis affecting the current practice of the sacrament of penance in Africa*. Dissatisfaction with the Christian rite of reconciliation has in our view contributed to the emergence of new forms of reconciliation, and in a second section we present some elements of these. We shall conclude with a brief analysis of these new practices within Africa's Christian communities.

1. THE QUESTIONS RAISED BY DISSATISFACTION

(a) A broader sense of sin

The normal experience of many priests, outside the eve of major feasts like Christmas and Easter, is to spend a long time in the confessional only to encounter children fresh from their catechism class and aged widows whose joints have been stiffened by arthritis and who groan when kneeling down and getting up again. The dialogue exchanged with these penitents shows at once that what is involved is merely a *routine* gone through so as to be able to go to communion the following day.

But has the active adult population not got anything to reproach itself with? The world they live in is interlaced with prohibitions and taboos, and their consciences are often keenly aware of what is wrong and not in keeping with the norms of society. It is thus not the awareness of sin that has become blunted: it is rather the *very idea of sin and conversion that needs to be re-adjusted*, not to lighten the demands of Christ but to make our peoples become aware of them by presenting them in categories accessible to them. Ought not the idea of sin to be broadened in our catechesis in Africa so as to be able to include, in our languages, all the categories of evil, including the evil that is brought about without the intention of committing it? Ought not the African list of sins to be integrated into that of Christianity? Observations like: 'I've sinned, but I haven't done anything wrong' speak volumes. Sin in Africa is essentially an evil that is committed or brought about against one's neighbour: rather than lamenting this overgrown social and community dimension, we should make use of it to catch up with God's plan for mankind, that of gathering together a holy brotherhood to praise his glory. Wronging one's neighbour will thus appear as opposing God's plan.

(b) More than preparation for communion

The sacrament of penance has most frequently been presented as a *preparation for going to communion*: just as one ironed one's shirt and trousers on Saturday night so as to be properly turned out when one went to Mass on Sunday, so one visited the confessional in order to be able to go to communion the next day. The link that was made between confession and Eucharist did not sufficiently bring to light the fact that the *sacrament of penance was a permanent necessity in life*, a reality that restored harmony within the society that forms the Church and within the universe. I have heard people say: 'I tell you, Father, that man was lucky because it was Saturday and I'd just been to confession; if it had been Monday he'd have felt my fist in his face.'

Priests lament the fact that communions are increasing while confessions are declining. Cannot this be explained among other things by the fact that in people's minds confession no longer holds the monopoly of assuring them that they are restored to God's grace? This role is more and more filled by other prayers or devotions, a little like the first centuries of the Church's history. Many of my parishioners continue to think that the prayer asking for forgiveness at the start of Mass can replace the sacrament of penance. 'Is God tied to the rite when it comes to forgiving?' they ask. I have done my best to explain that this prayer does not rank as a sacrament even if it can obtain God's forgiveness for people.

(c) Always in need of salvation

What is absolutely novel for our peoples is to present the human being *as a weak creature in whom good and evil do their work* and thus a being bound to mortify himself and to do penance in order to be able to attach himself to God and to rediscover his image and likeness. Our catechesis must insist on this point and underline that while the rediscovery of this image may begin in this world it is only fully achieved in the next, and that our ancestors were equally concerned about this process of rediscovery: the prohibitions and laws they have bequeathed to us must therefore be brought into harmony with the Christian rites of reconciliation to the extent that these prohibitions and laws are aimed at re-establishing the balance and harmony that have been broken between human beings and God and between human beings and the community he or she belongs to, between human beings and the cosmos. The only foundation for this harmony is to be found in God's plan for the world, a plan in which Jesus Christ is at the centre. Hence Christianity must make room for the African rites of reconciliation, which in their turn must admit of being directed towards Christ and his message. This double approach seems to me to be adopted in the various experiments we shall now describe.

2. VARIOUS EXPERIMENTS

(a) Cijiba

This is a region where a number of different traditional chiefs are disputing the leadership among themselves. To avoid becoming entangled in their domestic quarrels I asked the government authorities for an 'autonomous area' of twelve acres free from tribal law. Here are to be found the presbytery, the church, the schools, the maternity hospital and the dispensary, and living there are some teachers and other Catholics, making up about two hundred inhabitants in all. In withdrawing this area from the direct authority of the chiefs a way of settling conflicts within the community had to be established in advance. *Our guiding principle was to settle all our conflicts in the Christian way* so as to be able to give the entire population an example which would show that the Christian faith is the liberation of man, the power of life, the potential of love. It was in this context that rituals of reconciliation took shape.

When a quarrel breaks out between two individuals, the community leader calls the two parties together in the presence of two other 'elders' (i.e. older members of the community); he establishes the responsibility of each in the quarrel that has arisen; with the help of his advisers he pronounces judgment on the wrongs done and lays down a penalty and how amends should be made. They then agree on a day for reconciliation—and often it is the day when the community comes together for prayer. On this day proceedings begin with a reading from the Word of God; the community leader comments on this and then introduces the matter in hand; each of the two parties to the quarrel is allowed his or her say; the guilty party admits the wrong he or she has done and the injured party renounces revenge, spitting on the ground. As penalty the guilty party has brought tea and milk prepared in advance which he or she then distributes to the assembly. The two parties to the quarrel drink first, both from the same cup, and after them everyone else drinks. If the quarrel has caused significant damage, such as wounding or the loss of a chicken, a pig, or a goat, the community makes the guilty party promise to restore what has been lost, but already, as a pledge of his or her good faith, he or she is required to hand over half or a third of what is owed. This reconciliation is not sacramental, but the Christians rank it as high as, if not higher than, the sacrament.

(b) A group of religious

A priest presides: the meeting starts with readings interspersed with a penitential chant. The group is more select and intimate. After the gospel the priest comments in a way that raises questions. This is followed by a brief period of silence. Then the priest calls on each one to make his confession. The group forms a circle round the altar, and each member admits his wrong-doings and failings out loud. Once everyone has made his confession, a basin of water is brought in and placed on the altar. The celebrant blesses the water with one of the traditional formulae, asking that through the power of the Spirit the water may have the power to purify. After the water has been blessed each penitent washes his hands in it, saying: 'Lord, through your mercy grant that my sins may disappear as if drowned in water.' When everyone has done this the priest gives general absolution. A thanksgiving chant is then intoned, during which the celebrant takes the basin of water and goes to throw the dirty water outside, on the roof of the chapel. When he returns to the group he asks for a few minutes' silent prayer: this is followed by the Our Father, after which everyone is invited to exchange the kiss of peace and the celebration comes to an end.

(c) Reconciliation of a magician

We often encounter the problems raised by witchcraft. Formerly missionaries thought they could resolve the problem by classing it among 'vain beliefs and superstitions', but this merely had the effect of burying the embers under the ashes. This stage is over. Our catechesis has to recognise that the witch-doctor exists; he is the incarnation of evil; his evil spells are baleful; he is one of the 'strong ones' who know how to stimulate and channel the interaction of forces, but instead of using them for good the witch-doctor turns them into a disaster for his neighbour. This evil is not innate: there are not people who are born as witch-doctors, but they can be deceived by their heart without having wanted this. Traditional techniques made the witch-doctor spew his witchcraft out. Christians, however, have recourse to the Church to expel the evil that is within him from the man who is contaminated.

The first method was charismatic prayer, as exemplified by the practice of Archbishop Emmanuel Milingo in Zambia, of Fr Lufuluabo in Kasai, of Fr Kibwila in Kinshasa, and of Fr Kasongo in Shaba. Their ritual consists of the laying on of hands accompanied by prayer: sometimes holy water is also sprinkled.

The parish priest of Kabare in East Africa follows a different procedure. The Christians of the village and other sympathisers gather, while the priest withdraws for a time with the guilty person for an individual confession which is not followed by absolution. The guilty person then joins the assembly to confess his wrong-doing and to ask forgiveness for the wrongs he has done the community. As an earnest of his contrition and his determination not to succumb to evil again, he drops on the ground all the equipment used in his evil rites, such as a symbolic cord used to 'bind' his victims, a small pot for cooking human flesh. The priest asks the assembly: 'Do you want X to be reconciled with us?' The people answer: 'Yes, but provided he makes reparation.' The penitent then produces what he has prepared (usually a goat) and some maize beer. He gives these to the president of the assembly. If the penalty demanded is greater than the gifts he offers, he asks for and is granted time to make it up; but the reconciliation has already been accomplished. This leads into the celebration of the Eucharist followed by a meal for the whole community at which the goat or chickens offered in reparation are served.

(d) At childbirth

In our maternity hospitals a woman about to give birth finds herself on her own with the nurse or midwife, who usually does not have any family ties with her. If the woman reproaches herself for lacking respect for her parents-in-law, unfaithfulness to her husband, theft, or whatever, she confides in the nurse who prescribes a penalty which she pays on the spot. The fact of having confessed her wickedness to someone already forms a kind of restoration of order. The midwife says the Our Father with the woman and makes the sign of the cross.

(e) Independent Churches

In many Christian sects, confession is public but not always explicit or personalised: it is often followed by giving something up, such as total abstention from food and drink for one, two or three days, or prolonged prayer-vigils. Lutheran missionaries in Angola ask penitents to pay the penalty demanded by the heads of the family.

3. BRIEF ANALYSIS

What first strikes us about these experiments is the effort to create a *synthesis between the old and the new*. It would be interesting to recall the different types of reconciliation traditionally found in Black Africa: between two peoples, between two families, general reconciliation at a time of major events or disasters like war, epidemics, moving home, reconciliation in preparation for rites of healing, reconciliation of an individual with a community, of a man with his brother, his father, his mother, his wife, etc. These rituals can be found elsewhere.[2] Throughout, three elements recur: confession, the involvement of the community, and reparation.

(a) The community

Maintaining this element corresponds exactly to the Black African concept of the world as marked by *participation, with every creature linked to the life of others like intercommunicating vessels*. If life is diminished in one place the entire group is threatened, from the ancestors down to those living on the earth now. Hence, because wrong-doing is a disharmony introduced into life, it is capable of bringing about a chain-reaction. The wrong-doing of a single individual must be made good by the whole group: it is a 'social wrong'.[3] But the way in which this community is represented can vary according to each case. The different attempts at synthesis reported above have done this easily enough: the second one even deliberately breaks the canonical rules of the penitential liturgy by allowing general absolution in a select group in the absence of an emergency. These new rituals try to make a place for the *idea of forgiveness*, which is more absent than not from the traditional rites which emphasize above all the aspect of the restoration of order, the re-establishment of the social and cosmic balance that has been upset. This is particularly shown by the introduction of readings from the Bible and prayer to God. There is also an enlargement of the community: it is no longer a question of those sharing a common ancestor but also of all those who share in the new life they have received from Christ. It is the 'elder' of the community who presides, while associating with himself the 'elders' of the tribe or clan when they are present.

(b) Confession

The spoken word is a fundamental element in oral cultures. It is not simply a means and an instrument: it is *personified, it acts*. The confession shares in this dynamism of the spoken word. To say that one has done wrong is to go in the opposite direction from that which was bad and defective. But is it necessary for this confession to be public? African tradition does not always demand this: it is enough that it should be made, at least before the representatives of the community.

(c) Reparation, punishment, penalty

A penalty or fine is imposed or liable in all our old rites of reconciliation. Sometimes the two individuals concerned put their gifts together in proportion to the wrong each has done, and these are then given to the elders or consumed by the community present. This meal that follows is often a symbol of communion; it expresses and leads to communion; thus it often serves as the conclusion of the rites of reconciliation. Good examples of its integration are to be seen in cases (a) and (c) quoted above. The latter, where the Eucharist is celebrated at the conclusion of the reconciliation of a witch-doctor, could also be classed among rites of reconciliation demanding a sacrifice. This immolation of a victim is not to be understood in the sense of the collective expression of violence to be found in the works of René Girard. The dog that is killed or the woman who is buried alive (Ciyamba)[4] is not a victim on which the group loads all its sins but a life which the group sets up to watch over the covenant. The celebration of the Eucharist at the end of a rite of reconciliation sets up Christ as guarantor. To sum up: these are small steps, but they open up an immense horizon.

Translated by Robert Nowell

Notes

1. *Péché, pénitence et réconciliation* (Tradition chrétienne et culture africaine) (Kinshasa 1980).
2. V. Turner *Les Tambours d'affliction* (Paris 1972); L. V. Thomas and R. Luneau *Les Religions d'Afrique noire* (Paris 1981); Mbuyi Wenu Buila *Bankambua beetu* ('Our ancestors') (Kinshasa 1972) IV.
3. Tshiamalenga-Ntumba 'La Philosophie de la faute dans la tradition luba', in *Péché, pénitence et réconciliation* (Kinshasa 1980) pp. 132–134.
4. Mbuyi Wenu Buila, the work cited in note 2.

PART III

*Ecclesial and Theological
Traditions*

Cesare Giraudo

Confession of Sins in the Old Testament

1. THE CONFESSION OF SINS AS COVENANT SPEECH

CHRISTIANS, ESPECIALLY Catholics, often feel uncomfortable about
the confession of sins, largely because the penny catechism has accustomed
them to thinking of the *examination of conscience as the principal element in
conversion*. They concentrate all their attention on this examination, which
tends to become an exhaustive enquiry into the number of sins and a
scrupulous going-over of their circumstances, even when the sins are not
grave. The risk here is that they may easily lose sight of God and remain alone
with their sins. For the Old Testament believer on the other hand, to judge
from the confession formulas available to us, this risk did not arise.

*Sin in the Old Testament is always spoken about in terms of a relationship or
non-relationship*, of covenant and broken covenant.[1] When God and human
beings meet in the Old Testament, it is never a piecemeal affair; they always
meet in terms of their whole relationship and its profound consequences for
salvation history. Therefore when he commands Israel to enter into his
covenant, God does not give the command merely by using such expressions
as 'Serve me' or 'You must serve me'. Like an ancient Middle Eastern Great
King speaking to his vassals, God gives a long highly structured speech
relating the pre-history of the relationship, in terms of which he gives his
commandment. In the covenent formula found in Gen. 24:2–15, the
commandment given in vv. 14–15[2] would be inconceivable to people of the

85

ancient Middle Eastern biblical world without the foregoing historical section of vv. 2–13. The commandment is based on it and gets its juridical and theological weight from it.

Likewise when Israel does not live up to the covenant, God does not merely threaten her with expressions such as: 'You will die' or 'Go into exile'. He makes a long speech to his unfaithful partner, in which he goes over the past history of their relationship and then pronounces his condemnation. In his prophetic denunciation of Deut. 32:4–25, we see how the historical section (vv. 4–18), which compares the story of God's faithfulness to that of his vassal's unfaithfulness, leads to the condemnation in vv. 19–25. Without the historical recall, the condemnation would have no juridical weight.

And finally when Israel in exile reflects and becomes aware of her sin, she does not just ask for forgiveness through expressions such as 'Forgive, Lord!' or 'Renew your covenant'. Both in individual and common prayer Israel is aware of the need to offer God a *proper covenant speech*, in which she first confesses God's faithfulness and her own infidelity by recalling the relationship's past, and thence formulates her plea for forgiveness. In these pages we will point out the main lines of this covenant speech, which is the confession of sins, in order to bring out the underlying conversion theology as the tension of a relationship.

2. TWO WAYS OF CONFESSING SINS

If we want to understand the theological resonance of the Old Testament phrase 'confess sins', we must also consider its *correlative expression* 'confess the Lord'. The latter figures typically in Joshua's invitation to Achan, who has violated the anathema: 'My son, give glory to the Lord God of Israel and render *tôdâ* (RSV: praise; Italian text: confession) to him; and tell me now what you have done; do not hide it from me.' (Josh. 7:19).

Achan's confession begins at verse 20: 'Of a truth I have sinned against the Lord God of Israel, and this is what I did.' There follows the detailed account of his wrongdoings. Although fully understandable in the context of sacral law, the Achan episode is the extreme case, in which the covenant cycle, rigidly restricted to the single binary mode of relationship and non-relationship, has to conclude with the death of the sinner. As there is no possibility of real forgiveness in this story, it is difficult to insert it into salvation history.

However, Esd. 10:11 offers a positive epilogue. This is another case of an invitation to 'make a *tôdâ* (confession) to the Lord'. Here the expression invites the whole community to take part in the penitential prayer previously offered by the community's head alone (see Esd. 9:6–15) and prepares the homecomers to re-enter into the covenant through their sacral recognition of God's holiness and their wickedness. From covenant theology we know that sin recognised does *not* definitively close off the salvation cycle. On the contrary it opens the sinner to God, moves God to forgiveness and thus introduces the covenant cycle as an *infinite recurrence of the two phases of sin and grace.* As these alternate ceaselessly, they reveal to the vassal God's unbreakable will to save him.

Before we examine the two confession formularies, we must take a look at the semantic group *ydh/tôdâ* (confess/confession), used in the Old Testament to describe the attitude of the vassal on the point of being restored to his relationship with his Lord. This Semitic linguistic group, carried on in biblical Greek in the verbs *exomologeisthai* and *exagoreuein,* and particularly in the New Testament in the verb *eucharistein,*[3] can take two sorts of complement. In reference to a term signifying guilt, the verb means that the human partner recognises and *confesses his own sin*; in reference to God, on the other hand, the verb means that the human partner recognises and *confesses his Lord*, proclaiming this Lord's greatness and irrevocable will to save.

This is enough to allow us to glimpse the *theological richness of the covenant language.* However, the tendency to make the superior partner as great as possible, through the proclamation of his absolute fidelity and consequently to diminish the inferior partner through awareness of his sins, does not crush the latter, but tells him that everything his Lord is, he is for him.

(a) Talking to God in our own words

The confession of sins, like any other prayer formulary, takes the form of a *speech made to God.* In literary terms, it is articulated into a *historical section* (which is therefore expressed in the indicative mode) and a *petition section* (expressed in the imperative). In the indicative section the praying community, speaking through its leader, tells in cultic form the story of their relationship, a story of God's faithfulness and our unfaithfulness, his grace and our sin. Technically we call this the *anamnetic celebratory section* (marked thus:*), because here the praying community *celebrates* God i.e. 'confesses' and praises him, in an anamnesis or recall of the relationship's past. This first section, which is not a 'captatio benevolentiae' as a superficial reading might lead us to believe, *lays the logical and theological ground leading to the petition section.* Thus the recall or anamnesis of God's faithfulness, also revealed through the recollection of our unfaithfulness, enables the praying community to ask the Lord to intervene on a particular occasion in the life of his subjects and manifest again his faithfulness, which is the only guarantee of a return to him and possession of the land. Technically we call this imperative section the *epicletic section* (marked thus:**), because in it the cultic community makes its *epiclesis* or invocation to God.

Let us now look at this twofold articulation in the typical penitential prayer that we find in Neh. 9:6–37. The immediate context is described in verses 1–5. After verse 1 has related the outward behaviour characterising the penitential rite (assembly, fasting, sackcloth and dust), verse 2 states that they 'stood (in a sacral posture) and *confessed their sins* and the iniquities of their fathers.' Verse 3 divides the time dedicated to prayer into two parts, the second of which is the one that interests us here: 'they made confession and worshipped the Lord their God.'[4] Then, after the invitation in verse 5, there follows the penitential prayer. Because of its length we cannot quote it in full, so we confine ourselves to extracting certain significant expressions, which will enable the reader to gather its literary and theological movement.

6. *Thou art the Lord, thou alone; thou hast made the heaven ...
7. Thou art the Lord, the God who didst choose Abram ...
8. and didst make with him the covenant to give to his descendants the land ...
9. And thou didst see the affliction of our fathers in Egypt and hear their cry ...
10. and didst perform signs and wonders against Pharoah ...
11. And thou didst divide the sea before them ...
12. By a pillar of cloud thou didst lead them ...
13. Thou didst come down upon Mount Sinai ...
14. thou didst make known to them thy holy sabbath ...
15. Thou didst give them bread from heaven ...
16. But they and our fathers acted presumptuously ...
17. they refused to obey ...
    But thou art a God ready to forgive ... and didst not forsake them ...
18. Even when they had made for themselves a molten calf ...
19. thou in thy great mercies didst not forsake them ...
21. Forty years didst thou sustain them in the wilderness ...
22. And thou didst give them kingdoms and peoples ...
24. So the descendants went in and possessed the land ...
    ... so they ate, and were filled and became fat ...
26. Nevertheless they were disobedient and rebelled ...
27. Therefore thou didst give them into the hands of their enemies, who made them suffer; and in the time of their suffering they cried to thee ...
28. and many times thou didst deliver them according to thy mercies.
29. Yet they acted presumptuously and did not obey ...

30. Many years thou didst bear with them ...
31. in thy great mercies thou didst not make an end of them ... for thou art a gracious and merciful God.
32. **Now therefore, our God ... who keepest covenant ... let not all the hardship seem little to thee that has come upon us ... (and) our fathers ...
35. They did not serve thee ... in the large and rich land ...
36. Behold, we are slaves this day; in the land that thou gavest to our fathers ... behold, we are slaves.
37. And its rich yield goes to the kings whom thou hast set over us ... and we are in great distress.

In the *anamnetic-celebratory section* (vv. 6–31) of this exquisite historical prayer, we hear the cultic proclamation of the whole past history of the relationship, beginning with the remembrance of God's eternal oneness acting at the time of the creation (v. 6) and then later at the time of his choosing of Abraham (vv. 7–8). In vv. 9–15 this tale of salvation history takes up the story from the sufferings of their fathers in Egypt to the giving of the manna. Here the purpose of the historical proclamation is absolutely positive, because the undisputed protagonist of the relationship is the Lord, who sees, hears and works miracles for his vassal. But quite soon the horizon of this idyll darkens and in vv. 16–21 we hear about their fathers' presumptuousness and refusal to obey. Here the protagonist—this time with the role of the 'evildoer'—is Israel, while God for his part confines himself to forgiving, not forsaking and feeding his rebellious vassal.

In contrast vv. 22–25 return to the proclamation of God's faithfulness, which regains the active role. We see him personally involved in giving the land, whereas his children need do nothing but enter it, take possession of it and enjoy its fruits. However the sequence 'eat, become full, grow fat' (v. 25) intended to show the fulfilment of the promise is also the immediate prelude to the vassal's unfaithfulness (see Deut. 32:15). Vv. 26–31 dramatically oppose the actors on the stage, who now agree to share the role of protagonist: one intent on rebelling and acting presumptuously disobeying and after being punished, crying for mercy; the other intent on punishing and liberating, waiting patiently and refraining from finally short-circuiting the covenant cycle.

On the foundation of the sacral proclamation of this mysteriously interwoven twin story, arises the *epicletic section* (vv. 32–37). This is introduced by the *logico-temporal particle 'now therefore'*, which often functions as a link between the two sections. Formally the plea is confined to verse 32. The following verses are to make it more urgent and adds a mention of 'all the hardship that has come upon us'. At first sight the content of this petition might seem rather slight, or at least surprisingly modest. They merely ask God that 'the hardship may not seem little to you'. However if we consider this request in the light of the literary and theological dynamic of the covenant structure, in which the *protasis in the indicative* is the juridical basis of the *apodosis in the imperative*, we recognise in the latter the imperious cry of the vassal who 'humbly enjoins'[5] his Lord to intervene in his present trial, restore the relationship and give him back the land. For the land he is standing on is no longer the land of his vassal service. It is a land of slavery, which imperturbably continues to produce fruits which are not for him. In its perfectly articulated literary and thematic structure, the penitential prayer of Nehemiah 9 reveals the theological 'road' of conversion. The trial of the present moment (vv. 36–37) forces the praying people to say 'we' in a way which associates them with the afflictions of their fathers (v. 27). These are then related to the punishment inflicted on successive sins, the many refusals to obey and the vassal's presumptuous behaviour, growing fat on the land given to him as a concession and impatient to make its fruits his own by right. *Thus hardship reveals sin and in turn sin recognised makes the unfaithful vassal rediscover his inescapable relationship to God.* Just as in hard times he is forced to say 'we' again, this leads him also to say 'you' to the partner of the ancient convenant. It is significant to point out how the vassal's 'we', which is the dramatic culmination of the epicletic section (v. 37), parallels the repeated 'yous' addressed to God which purposely open and close the anamnetic-celebratory section (vv. 6 and 31).

(*b*) Talking to God in our words and God's words

As well as the penitential prayer we have analysed in Nehemiah 9, which we may call simple in its basic two-part structure, there is *another form* whose characteristics we will try to describe from the example of the confession in Num. 14:13–19. This is Moses' prayer to God who has decided to exterminate his rebellious people and make of Moses a great nation otherwise. Here is the text:

13. *Then the Egyptians will hear of it, for thou didst bring up this people in thy might from among them,
14. and they will tell the inhabitants of this land. They have heard that thou, O Lord, art in the midst of this people; for thou O Lord, art seen face to face, and thy cloud stands over them and thou goest before them, in a pillar of cloud by day and in a pillar of fire by night.

15. Now if thou dost kill this people as one man, then the nations who have heard thy fame will say,
16. 'Because the Lord was not able to bring this people into the land which he swore to give them, therefore he has slain them in the wilderness.'

17. **And now, I pray thee, let the power of the Lord be great as thou hast promised, saying,
18. '*The Lord is slow to anger and abounding in steadfast love, forgiving iniquity and transgression but he will by no means clear the guilty, visiting the iniquity of fathers upon children, upon the third and upon the fourth generation.*'
19. Pardon the iniquity of this people, I pray thee, according to the greatness of thy steadfast love, and according as thou hast forgiven this people from Egypt even until now.

Considerations of literary structure emerging from the observation of a large number of penitential prayers, enable us to regard vv. 13–16 as the *anamnetico-celebratory section* of this highly circumstantial prayer. Although the whole section is permeated with history, the celebratory aspect (i.e. the confession and praising of the Lord) needs to be pointed out, because it is transposed into the mouth of the Egyptians. Instead of saying in verse 13: 'You are the one who brought us out ...' Moses, conducting his prayer with acute pedagogical insight,[6] says: 'The Egyptians have heard that you brought out ...' The logic of the argument becomes plain in vv. 15–16, which predicts what the nations will say if the Lord fulfils his threat to destroy the people. The specific function of v. 16 can be understood better after we have considered verse 18, to which it is neatly opposed.

With the support of the *logico-temporal particle 'and now'* we pass to the *epicletic section* (vv. 17–19), which is expressed in the pleas in verse 17: 'Let the power of the Lord be great' and verse 19: 'pardon according to the greatness of thy steadfast love'. Here a new element is introduced. In order to gain maximum theological credibility, the epicletic section in this prayer splits into two *like a tree prepared for grafting*, and inserts God's own words most suited to the present situation.

We can use this *grafting metaphor* to show the force of this particular insertion into the prayer. As in a plant the body to be grafted on is by definition foreign to its host, so the pericope in verse 18 is originally a foreign body in Moses' prayer. It comes from Exod. 34:6–7 where God passes before Moses, revealing himself whereas previously he has been known only through his attributes. And just as the grafted plant at first suffers a traumatic moment because of the foreign body that has been introduced but then quickly shows new vigour, so once the foreign literary body has been grafted on and accepted into Moses' prayer, it confers a new theological vitality to the whole and scriptural theological strength to the petition. By grafting God's own words into their prayer, the people or individual praying reminds God in a singularly effective way i.e. in his own words, of his promise made in ancient times about troubles to come in the future, that future which has now become the troubled present. No sooner has Moses reminded God in God's own words of his habitual slowness to anger and steadfast love, than he hastens to use this to plead for the defence in verse 19, on the grounds of this very steadfastness. In technical terms, we may call the literary device of the insertion of God's word to support the argument for forgiveness, a form of embolism or *literary grafting*.[7]

In the light of verse 18 we are now in a better position to understand the function of verse 16. Here Moses in his prayer seriously considers the possibility of Israel's extermination and anticipates what their enemies will say if God's promise is not kept. Thus the enemies' retort, which is formally quoted as a negative embolism, provokes a crescendo of expectation that God will fulfil his promise.

Thus if we compare the *simple structure* of the confession of sins in Neh. 9 with the *embolistic structure* of Num. 14, we find that the latter is both more complex and richer. For as well as the common two-part structure, in which the celebratory anamnesis of the past is the juridical foundation of the petition, the embolistic dynamic of the petition in Numbers gives it a further theological foundation. The embolism or literary grafting introduces a *new element, the words of God himself*, which proclaim in advance that the prayer will be heard. The person praying wants to give his petition maximum theological force, so he searches the scriptures, that archive of God's words, for the salvation oracle which best fits his particular prayer. Once he has found it, he inserts it textually into his prayer formulation, so that when God hears his own words of forgiveness returning to him as a prayer, his *reḥamîm* (fatherly guts) churn with emotion.

3. FROM LEX ORANDI TO LEX CREDENDI. TWO CONSIDERATIONS ON THE OLD TESTAMENT THEOLOGY OF SIN

The literary form of confession of sins, which we have examined in two actual prayers is not just literary. It is a *cultic act and as such the bearer of theology*. We know that the Old Testament believer (and after him the Christian believer during the first millenium, who was limited to the environment of sacramental experience) was well aware of the limits of pure speculation and preferred to do his theology by praying. He believed as he prayed and to the extent that the prayed.[8] Therefore we conclude this article on the Old Testament idea of sin with two reflections arising from this 'lex orandi'.

(a) Confession of sin is openness to God

We can only understand the theological breadth of the confession of sin in the Old Testament if we take into account the *semantic breadth* of the linguistic group: *ydh/tôdâ* (confess/confession).[9] In this sacral context *'confessing our own unfaithfulness' immediately means 'confessing the superiority of the ever-faithful partner'* and vice versa. As a cultic act, the behaviour of the human partner who confesses is neither a self-damaging contemplation of his own sinful state nor a disembodied contemplation of God's holiness. It is always a proclamation in an existing relationship of the Other's absolute superiority, which emerges from the joyful and painful comparison of him with our sinful humanity. At the point when Israel resolves to confess its sin, it realises that the ultimate object of this confession is not 'its' sin, but the Lord, who alone is able to restore the convenant relationship.

In the 'lex orandi' sin acknowledged is a revelation of God's otherness and thus, in itself, covenant and grace. Secure in forgiveness already promised, the sinner at the culmination of his confession quite often reminds God of God's promise to forgive, as if to activate God's unbreakable will to save him.[10]

(b) Confession of sins is openness to history

In the two penitential prayers we have examined, and in many others analysed elsewhere, to which we refer the reader,[11] we can see how the person praying, after enumerating his own sin, is immediately concerned to place his confession in the broader context of past infidelities and thus of God's saving interventions in the history of his fathers. This continual referral from the present situation back into history is a constant in the Old Testament doctrine of sin and grace.

In other words, the faith of the Old Testament believer leads to a continual *displacement of a purely moral conception of sin by a theological one*. The idea that individual and community—through an assessment which must be as objective and dispassionate as possible—force themselves to weigh up their sins (in the plural!) gives way to the theological conception, in which individual and community place sin (in the singular!) in a global context of their relationship with God. Of course there is a time when the moral assessment of sin is necessary, because it forces us to think about which way our life is going and refines our conscience so that we try to behave better in future. But this moral assessment-time should be limited. If it goes on too long, we risk becoming enclosed within the narrow bounds of our own guilt, producing dangerous states of anxiety and scrupulosity. However there is no time limit for the theological assessment of sin. The longer it goes on the more it opens us up to God and the constant historical manifestations of his relationship with us.

We conclude by recalling the paradoxical case of openness, which we found in the penitential speech in Numbers 14. When the Lord, going by the text, seems to close himself off on a point by point and therefore strictly moral judgment of Israel's sin, Moses, who has taken over God's mind, resolutely intervenes and with an 'ad hominem' argument forces God to open up again to their common experience of salvation history 'from Egypt until now' (Num. 14:19). What is paradoxical about this text is the fact that the subject who has to open, through a progressive realisation of the mysterious reality which is sin, is *God himself* and the openness is to humanity and history.

Translated by Dinah Livingstone

Notes

1. The idea of the covenant can be considered as the key to the whole message of the Old Testament.

2. For a deeper study of the texts simply quoted here or only partially analysed, see my study *La struttura letteraria della preghiera eucaristica* (Rome 1981).

3. See *ibid.* pp. 260–269. The equivalence between *eucharistein* and *ydh* is confirmed by the Syriac.

4. The object of this second recurrence of the verb is the Lord. (See the work cited in note 2, p. 128, n. 6).

5. When we speak of 'humbly enjoining' or a 'beseeching command' the juxtaposition of the two apparently opposite notions is not accidental. On the analogy of the covenant structure, which seesaws between commandment and pleading. See the work cited in note 2, pp. 14–16, 109.

6. In his prayer Moses is teaching God.

7. For the notion of *embolism* meaning 'literary grafting' (in Greek *to embolon* is a graft on a tree) and for the developments of this literary device in Jewish and Christian liturgy (eucharistic prayer and other sacramental prayers), see my article 'Le Récit de l'institution dans la prière eucharistique a-t-il des antécédents?' in *NRT* 106 (1984) 513–536.

8. Obviously the Christian priority given to the 'lex orandi' over the 'lex credendi' already exists in the Old Testament. The criticisms of G. von Rad's theory of the 'historic creed' confirms this. In fact what has been proposed as a summary of the

ancient faith of Israel and the editorial basis of the primitive scriptural 'corpus', is just the historical section of the cultic formularies circling round the structure of the covenant: Deut. 26:5–7; Josh. 24:2–13; Deut. 32:4–18; Neh. 9:6–31 etc. (see *La struttura* pp. 44–50).

9. The observations on the theology of confession we have made in the light of the semantic group *ydh/tôdâ* are also valid even when these terms do not in fact occur in a formulary (see the work cited in note 2, pp. 16–163).

10. The embolistic dynamic of the confession of sins, which we have purposely considered in a less known formulary (Num. 14) is widespread in all Old Testament prayer, and in Jewish and Christian prayer as a whole. With reference to the latter, we note that the use of such embolisms is common in a good number of both Eastern and Western formularies for the administration of the sacrament of penance (see my article in *NRT* 106 (1984) 526, n. 28; 527–528.

11. See the work cited in note 2, pp. 81–177.

Frans van de Paverd

Testimonies from the Christian East to the Possibility of Self-Reconciliation

1. THE ORIGIN OF CONFESSION

WHENEVER A Jew or a pagan wanted to enter the Church, he was not required to confess the sins of his past life before being admitted to the catechumenate or to full community with the Church. At a 'second penance', a convert was in fact expected to confess his sin if it had remained secret. Tertullian († after 220) was acquainted with the penitent's practice of making his concrete *faux pas* or at least his guilt known.[1] This distinction between *offences that had been committed before baptism and sins committed after embodiment in the Church* was probably ultimately based on the insight that the Church did not have the authority to judge outsiders, but was authorised to judge its own members (see 1 Cor. 5:12).

When a baptised person sins, his mode of behaviour is not simply an infringement of the inviolability of his fellow-man who is created in God's image and likeness, but also an offence against the expectations that the Church is permitted to have with regard to its members on the basis of their baptismal promises. By transgressing the law of Christ to a serious extent, a baptised person to some degree *excludes himself* from the Church, alienating himself from the Church. Having become an alien in this way, he cannot admit himself again without further ado to the Church. He has to ask, as it were, for the door to be opened to admit him. On the other hand, because the claims of the Church are also violated when a brother or sister fails, the community

96

acquires a right to forgiveness. In the case of secret sins, it can only exercise this right when the guilty person makes his going astray known.

A certain conception of the unicity of baptism may perhaps also have played a part in this. Christians were convinced that, by baptism, all the sins of a person's past life were cancelled out, as it were with the stroke of a pen. This forgiveness (*aphesis*) was, however, an unrepeatable event (see Heb. 6:4–6; 10:26–27). For a sin committed after baptism, such a purely gratuitous gift was no longer available. Then a satisfaction, in the form of penance, was expected of the convert. This conception is particularly prominent in the teaching of Cyprian († 258).[2] The degree and the manner of the penance could only be determined by the Church. This also presupposes, in the case of secret sins, a confession. Seen from this point of view, the convert could not satisfy this requirement simply by recognising his guilt—he had to confess his concrete act. Only in this way could a penance that was appropriate to his sin be imposed on him.

However the emergence of confession has to be explained, the Christian East provides testimonies to the possibility that a *sinner may reconcile himself with the community without any special intervention on the part of the Church*. These testimonies cannot be included under a single heading. I shall therefore consider each one in turn in order to see whether they are or are not relevant.

2. TESTIMONIES TO THE POSSIBILITY OF SELF-RECONCILIATION

(a) It is part of the very essence of the Eucharist that it is only possible to participate worthily in it if one is living *at peace with one's fellow human beings*. That is why it was a general practice in the East to send away those who had something against their neighbour before the eucharistic prayer (see Matt. 5:23). By behaving irreconcilably towards one's neighbour, then, one excluded oneself from the community. There is, however, no evidence anywhere that a special intervention on the part of the Church was required in this case for the person's re-admission to the community. It was apparently sufficient for him to restore peace with his fellow-man for him to reconcile himself with the Church.

(b) Confession is not mentioned anywhere in the six books of the *Didascalia apostolorum* (beginning of the third century A.D.).[3] The second book is devoted to the tasks of the bishop, to whom it is made very clear that he should readmit to the community every (public) sinner whom he has excluded from the Church after his conversion. If the author of the document had been familiar with confession, one would certainly expect an indication from him of how the bishop should behave when a member of his community had confessed his sins to him.

(c) A remarkable text is found in the fourth canon of the Synod of Neocaesarea (314 A.D.): 'When a man intends to sleep with a woman because he desires her, but this intention is not realised, he appears to have been saved by grace.' This pronouncement implies that the frustrated intention does not need to be confessed. It would seem that the Fathers of the Synod respected the principle: *de internis Ecclesia non judicat*.[4]

(d) Basil of Caesarea and Gregory of Nyssa respected another principle, namely: *nulla poena sine lege*. If no law or no canon had been defined which specified penance for a certain offence by the 'Fathers', that is, their predecessors, a bishop could not impose a punishment on his own initiative. It can be demonstrated that confession was not required for such a 'non-canonical sin'.[5]

Do the testimonies mentioned under (c) and (d) above really prove that it was possible for a sinner to reconcile himself with the Church by conversion alone? Gregory writes that, of the sins that arise from covetousness, only theft, violation of tombs and church-robbery can be regarded as complaints, because the Fathers prescribed a penance for these offences alone. All other forms of greed were not taken seriously.[6] It is therefore possible to assert that all sins for which there were no canons prescribing penance were not subjectively experienced as 'mortal sins'. This means that there was no longer any awareness of the meaning of the liturgical practice mentioned under (a) above—assuming that this also existed in Cappadocia—and that the implication of such texts as Matt. 5:23–24; 6:12, 15; 18:36; Mark 11:25 and Luke 11:4 had, in any case, been forgotten. Both Basil and Gregory name, as examples of sins that were excluded from confession and penance, not only drunkenness, boastfulness, covetousness and desire for profit (see Col. 3:5; Eph. 5:5; 1 Tim. 6:10) and particularly usury and the obtaining of interest (see, for example, Exod. 22:25), but also all expressions of aggression (that is, as Gregory observes, with the exception of murder, for which there was a severe penance), scorn, envy, hatred, resentment, conflict and contentious and vengeful dispositions.[7]

(e) John Chrysostom never ceases to call on his listeners to be converted and to confess their sins. He never urges them, however, to reveal their misdeeds to the bishop or another member of the clergy. He says quite explicitly that he does not want to make them feel obliged to entrust their sins to human beings. It is *enough for them to show their wounds to God alone* and to ask him for a remedy. He makes his point of view clear both in his Antiochian and in his Constantinopolitan writings. It is not necessary to reproduce the texts in which his view is expressed in this article. J. Quasten provides two eloquent quotations in his *Patrology*, the first taken from the Antiochian period (*Hom. contra Anomaeos* 5; *PG* 48, 745) and the second from the Constantinopolitan period (*Hom. in Heb* 9, 5; *PG* 63, 81). It would not be difficult to add to these two texts. Quasten also points out that, in his books on the priesthood (*De sacerdotio*), Chrysostom lists seventeen tasks, but that hearing confessions is not included among them.[8]

We should not infer from the fact that Chrysostom taught his congregations that it was sufficient for them to recognise their sins in the presence of God alone that public penance was unknown in the churches of Antioch and Constantinople. In that respect, they were fully in accordance with all other local churches.[9] The only difference was that, in Antioch and Constantinople, the class of penitents consisted simply of the following persons: sinners who were caught red-handed, those whose guilt had been proved after they had been accused by third parties and members of the community whose way of life had caused public scandal.[10]

Chrysostom's view of confession was not based on a lack of insight into the ecclesial dimension of sin. Like others, he was also convinced that a baptised person whose attitude was in conflict with the holiness of the Church itself excluded himself *ipso facto* from the *communio*. He outlines this view very clearly in his homilies on David and Saul (*Hom. de Davide et Saule* 3, 1–2; *PG* 54, 695–7). Here he states that an unconverted sinner who is present outwardly at the solemnities in the Church is in fact further removed from the community than the penitent, who is not admitted to participation in communion, but who already has the prospect of full reconciliation (*PG* 54, 695). According to Chrysostom, then, it would seem that a sinner who has not been excluded officially from the Church, but who has only separated himself from the Church by his own behaviour can reconcile himself with the community by recognising his guilt in the presence of God alone. In such a case, there is no need for a special intervention on the part of the hierarchy. It would seem that the convert was able to assume *a priori* as a datum that the Church was disposed to forgive him.

(f) Theodore of Mopsuestia was a contemporary and friend of John Chrysostom. He also worked in the same (Roman) diocese of Syria. All the same, Theodore taught in his *Catechetical Sermons*[11] very clearly that, when a baptised person had committed a 'great sin' (*Hom.cat.* 16, 42; p. 599), he had to confess that sin to the bishop.[12] In a commentary on 1 Cor. 11:33–34, however, he says something different.[13] The text in question forms the conclusion to an exhortation to frequent communion. Consciousness of our unworthiness, Theodore says, should not prevent us from participating in communion. The only valid reason that the believer has for not participating is if he has made himself guilty of those sins, the committing of which will prevent him from inheriting the kingdom of God (see 1 Cor. 6:9–10; Gal. 5:21; Eph. 5:5). It is only suitable for a sinner of this kind to take part in the Eucharist after he has been converted. If, however, a believer tries to live as a good Christian, it is wrong for him to refrain from taking part and receiving communion because of his sinfulness, which is an inevitable part of our human condition.

It is even more wrong not to take part because forgiveness is given to us in the Eucharist. Theodore insists that 'it is reasonable that everything that has fallen to our lot through the death of Christ should also be made a reality by the symbols of his death'. He then concludes: 'So that I venture to assert that, if someone has committed even a serious sin, but has decided henceforth to refrain from all forms of unsuitable behaviour and to practise virtue by living according to the law of Christ and then takes part in the mysteries in the full conviction of receiving forgiveness for everything, he will in no way be disappointed in his faith.'

(g) The church historian Socrates († after 439) tells a racy story that is reputed to have led to the abolition of the office of penance presbyter.[14] This episode is also reported in the *Church History* of Socrates' contemporary Sozomen, who took it over from his colleague and enriched it with a number of his own additions.[15] According to Socrates, when Nectarius was the Bishop of Constantinople (381–397 A.D.), a noble lady came to see the penance presbyter and confessed one by one all the sins that she had committed since her baptism. The presbyter commanded the lady to fast and to pray without ceasing. She, however, continued with her confession and accused herself of another offence. She said that a deacon had slept with her. The result of this particular confession was that the deacon was excluded from the Church. The incident, however, had a further consequence: it caused a great disturbance among the people, who were outraged not only by what had happened, but also by the fact that the Church had been discredited. One Eudaimon, 'a presbyter of the Church and an Alexandrian by birth', therefore advised Bishop Nectarius to abolish the office of penance presbyter 'and to permit everyone to take part in the mysteries according to the judgment of his own conscience'. It was only in that way that the Church could remain exempt from calumny.

This story has greatly perplexed many scholars. It is not free from incongruities and historical impossibilities. So much, however, is quite clear: it presupposes the *absence of the practice of confession in Constantinople*. Socrates and Sozomen confirm in their historical works what we have already learned from Chrysostom.

(h) A canon that is of interest in connection with our subject has been ascribed to Timothy I of Alexandria (380–385).[16] He answers the question:

'What is suitable for someone who secretly commits a sin and, although he is ashamed of it, does not confess it?' The translation of this question is not entirely without difficulties, but the general significance of it is clear enough. It amounts to the fact that, when someone has secretly committed a sin and is then converted, keeps God's commandments and gives alms, 'God also forgives him'.

The point of departure taken by the person who asked this question and evoked this answer was clearly that confession formed the normal introduction to reconciliation. (Pseudo-)Timothy, however, asserts that, when someone does not, for some reason, confess his secret sins, his conversion expressed in the concrete will nonetheless move God to forgiveness.

(i) One last testimony comes from a much later period, namely the end of the twelfth century, but I include it because it demonstrates that the conviction still prevailed at that time that *even serious sins could be forgiven without confession*. Peter Chartophylax, who expressed this view, was the archivist of the Patriarch of Constantinople. He held, then, a position that was much more important than that of a simple librarian.[17] Using a literary genre that was very popular at the time in Byzantium, he expresses his opinion concerning various points in answers to a series of questions. He also provides solutions to problems concerning confession.[18] The answer that he gives to the question as to whether it is good for us to confess our sins to spiritual men is that it is certainly good and useful, but only when it is done in the presence of discerning confessors. 'When you find a spiritual and experienced man who is able to heal you, confess your sins to him without shame and with faith, as though you were confessing to the Lord and not to a man.'[19]

This statement, of course, raises the question as to what should be done if no competent spiritual man can be found. The author's reply is: 'Confess your sins in that case to God, in his presence alone, condemning yourself and, following the example of the tax collector (see Luke 18:13), saying: "Our God, you know that I am a sinner and unworthy of all forgiveness, but save me for the sake of your mercy." '

Finally, there is this question: 'When I confess my sins to God, must I then call to mind every sin that I have ever committed and enumerate them all?' Peter's answer is as follows: 'Certainly not! And especially not if you have sinned with your body and by unchastity (*porneia*). After all, as soon as you call this or that sin to mind, your soul is defiled. For that reason it is good to say, following the example of the tax collector: "God, be merciful to me, a sinner." ' It is clear from this last answer that Peter did not exclude sins that were generally regarded as serious.

It is also obvious from Peter's recommendations that an *important change had, in the course of time, taken place in the person of the confessor.* Originally, it had been the bishop who, by virtue of his responsibility for the holiness and the credibility of the community, had been the most suitable figure to act as confessor in the community and to judge with regard to exclusion and readmission. According to Peter, however, confessors should be *pneumatici.* In other words, they should be men who, because of a charismatic ability to discern, were capable of perceiving in each individual case what therapy should be applied here and now. In Peter's questions and answers, the Church aspect of sin and reconciliation is thrust completely into the background. Attention is focused exclusively on the personal salvation of the individual penitent. The confessor is no longer the Church's representative—he represents God himself.

3. AN AFTER-THOUGHT

It should be clear from what I have said above that even those authors who have recognised the importance of confession have also emphasised its relativity. *Only conversion is essential.* Even more testimonies of the kind that I have cited would undoubtedly be brought to light in a systematic examination of Byzantine theological literature. It seems to me, however, that the practice in Antioch and Constantinople to which Chrysostom bears witness is of special interest. It demonstrates—and the same is also clear from the *Didascalia apostolorum*—that the absence of auricular confession does not in any sense imply a lack of that procedure which later came to be called either— misleadingly—the 'sacrament of confession' or the 'sacrament of penance' or—by a name that is preferable—the 'sacrament of reconciliation'.

A discussion about the meaning of confession is not the same as a debate about the importance of the procedure of reconciliation. If confession and the sacrament of reconciliation amounted in fact to the same thing, then those who wish to discuss the meaning of confession would be diametrically opposed to the theologians of the early Church who engaged in polemics with the Montanists, Novatians and other rigoristic tendencies with the aim of perpetuating the possibility of at least a '*second* penance'. Doubting the right of a Church procedure of reconciliation is just as absurd as disputing the meaning and importance of baptism. The question that can be debated is not whether sins should or should not be confessed, *but in what cases an official reconciliation with the Church is offered.* It seems obvious to me that a baptised person, who has publicly removed himself from the Church or whose behaviour has been the cause of the Church's publicly placing itself at a distance from him, should be given the possibility of rehabilitating himself publicly and of straightening things out with the community.

Another question is whether, if a believer has not publicly excluded himself from the *communio*, the community should insist on having the unChristian behaviour of that person revealed to it in the person of its leader or his delegates, so that it can explicitly give forgiveness, whether conditional or unconditional. If this question is answered positively, we are bound to conclude that confession is indispensable. At the same time, however, it is also possible to ask oneself whether the gain that may result from a demand of this kind outweighs the loss that may go with it.

In this context, it may be helpful to add this after-thought. However much a person's way of life may be at variance with the holiness of the Church, the bond created by baptism cannot be broken. Even baptised persons who have been excluded from the *communio* continue to some extent to be members of the Church, although they may be 'suffering members who have gone astray'. This means that, as long as a member of the Church is cut off, the whole body is mutilated.[20] That is why it is possible to assert that it is opportune for the building up of the whole body, that the Church should in certain circumstances, in the case of secret sins, waive its right to explicit forgiveness. One of the circumstances that can be included here is the case in which a baptised believer who has separated himself from the community by his unworthy behaviour is later converted, but is not allowed to participate fully in the life of the Church because he does not experience confession as a liberating event, but regards it as a burden.

Translated by David Smith

Notes

1. H. Vorgrimler *Busse und Krankensalbung* (*Handbuch der Dogmengeschichte* IV/3) (Freiburg, Basle and Vienna 1978) p. 45.

2. H. Vorgrimler, the work cited in note 1, at p. 56.

3. F. X. Funk *Didascalia et Constitutiones apostolorum* I (Paderborn 1905; Turin 1970) pp. 1–384.

4. See F. van de Paverd 'The Matter of Confession according to Basil of Caesarea and Gregory of Nyssa' *Studi albanologici, balcanici, byzantini et orientali in onore di Giuseppe Valentini S.J.* (*Studi albanesi, studi e testi* VI) (Florence 1986) pp. 285–294. Cited below as 'The Matter'.

5. 'The Matter' pp. 285–291.

6. *Epist.can.* canon 6 (*PG* 45, 232D–233B); and see 'The Matter' p. 287.

7. See Basil *De jud. Dei* 7 (*PG* 31, 669A); *Hom in Ps 32,2* (*PG* 29, 325D–328D); see

'The Matter' pp. 290f.; Gregory *Epist. can.* canon 1 (*PG* 45, 225B); see 'The Matter' p. 291, n. 32; canon 5 (229CD); canon 6 (233B).

8. J. Quasten *Patrology* III (Utrecht and Antwerp 1963) pp. 478–479; see B. Altaner and A. Stuiber *Patrologie* (Freiburg, Basle and Vienna 1978) pp. 329f.

9. See F. van de Paverd 'Zur Geschichte der Messliturgie in Antiocheia und Konstantinopel' *OrChrA* 187 (Rome 1970) 184–198 (Antioch) and 453–460 (Constantinople).

10. See 'The Matter' p. 293 and *ibid.* n. 39.

11. R. Tonneau and R. Devréesse *Les Homélies catéchétiques de Théodore de Mopsueste* (*Studi e testi* 145) (Vatican City 1949).

12. See I. Oñatibia 'La doctrina de Teodoro de Mopsuestia sobre la penitencia eclesiastica' *Kyriakon. Festschrift für J. Quasten* I (Münster 1970) 427–440; see also J. Quasten, the work cited in note 8, pp. 422f.

13. See K. Staab *Pauluskommentar aus der griechieschen Kirche* (Münster 1933) p. 189.

14. *Hist. eccl.* 5, 19 (*PG* 67, 613A–620A).

15. *Hist. eccl.* 7, 16 (*PG* 67, 1457C–1464A); *Griechische christliche Schriftsteller* 50 (J. Bidez and G. C. Hansen) pp. 322, 17–324, 15.

16. *Responsio canonica* 35; I. B. Pitra *Juris ecclesiastici graecorum historia et monumenta* I (Rome 1864) p. 637.6.

17. For the person and the office of Peter Chartophylax, see H. G. Beck *Kirche und theologische Literatur im byzantinischen Reich* (*Handbuch der Altertumswissenschaft* XII, 2, 1) (Munich 1954) pp. 659 and 109ff.

18. *PG* 119, 1098.

19. The question and answer are also handed down under the name of Anastasius Sinaites († after 700); see *PG* 89, 369D–372A. For the series 'Questions and Answers' that are attributed to this author, see Beck, the work cited in note 17, p. 444.

20. See Polycarp of Smyrna *Epist. ad Phil* 11, 4.

Frank Senn

The Confession of Sins in the Reformation Churches

1. CONFESSION AND ABSOLUTION IN THE THEOLOGY AND PRACTICE OF MARTIN LUTHER (1483–1546)

THE REFORMATION was officially launched on 31 October 1517 when Martin Luther posted *Ninety-Five Theses* concerning the sale of indulgences on the door of the Castle Church in Wittenberg. In the development of indulgences[1], it remained a constant part of Church teaching that in benefitting either the living or the dead, they aided only those who were united with the church in charity. However, in Luther's time the trafficking in indulgences was undoubtedly abusive. The indulgence which came to Luther's attention was authorised jointly by Pope Leo XIII and archbishop Albrecht of Mainz and Magdeburg for the financing of the construction of St Peter's Basilica in Rome.[2] This jubilee indulgence provided for the remission of all penalties for the dead in purgatory without confession or contribution on the part of the living who applied indulgences to the dead. Luther had already warned the people of the danger of being misled by indulgences and of the necessity of sincere repentance.[3] In the *Ninety-Five Theses* he developed the idea that penance is not a mechanical act but an *inner attitude reflecting a life of repentance*.[4] He objected to the financing of St Peter's through the sale of indulgences, denied that the pope had any authority over purgatory and asserted that indulgences induce a false sense of religious security and thereby imperil salvation.

Luther continued to develop his views on the theology and practice of penance during the years 1518–1520 in the light of his *theology of justification by faith*.[5] He dismissed the medieval division of the sacrament of penance into four parts—contrition, confession, absolution, and satisfaction. Both contrition and satisfaction contribute to works-righteousness by leading one to believe that one truly can be sorry for one's sins and atone for them. One should trust not in one's own remorse but in the promise of God to forgive sinners for Christ's sake, and performing works of satisfaction after absolution undermines confidence in the word of God.

Christians should be taught to turn to God in faith, trusting his promise to forgive sinners for Christ's sake, and be assured of forgiveness from God himself. But because faith is often weak, it is advantageous to have a Christian brother or sister to confess to, and to hear from this person God's word of forgiveness. This person need not be a priest; indeed, the clergy have no monopoly on absolution. Since God alone forgives sins, the important thing is to trust his word. But faith needs to hear this word through the voice of a brother or sister in Christ, and the pastor may appropriately serve in the role of confessor since he is called and ordained as a minister of the word and sacraments. Nevertheless, confession should be free and one should confess only those sins which torment the conscience; one cannot know all of one's sins.

Luther wanted to retain private confession. While he was sequestered in the Wartburg after the Diet of Worms (1521), Andreas Karlstadt abolished confession before communion as a part of his iconoclastic campaign. Luther returned to Wittenberg in 1522 to restore order by preaching eight sermons in eight days. The last sermon defended the value of private confession and pleaded that Christians not be drawn away from this means of grace.[6] In the years thereafter he sought to shore up the practice of confession among evangelical Christians. He provided an Exhortation to Confession in *The Large Catechism* (1529)[7] and a form for Confession and Absolution in *The Small Catechism* (1529).[8] While still refusing to make confession obligatory, Luther held that the law of God will drive people to a knowledge of their sins and to confession. In the word of absolution they will hear the Gospel of forgiveness applied personally and directly to them, and they are to believe that when the absolution is spoken by the pastor the sinner is forgiven by God in heaven. As Bertil Werkström observes, relating confession and absolution to the Word of God as both law and Gospel puts an end to all idea of merit in connection with confession.[9] Luther vacillated on whether to regard *confession and absolution as a sacrament*, but it was clearly a means of grace and as such should be highly regarded.

Luther emphasised the word of absolution in the confession of sins. This should not be interpreted as 'pure nominalism' on Luther's part.[10] Rather, it relates to his understanding of the Gospel as 'forgiveness of sins, life, and salvation'.[11] In his grace, God has given many forms of absolution: the preaching of the word in which God's forgiveness is proclaimed, baptism, the sacrament of the altar, and the office of the keys. To these Luther added, in the *Smalcald Articles*, 'the mutual conversation and consolation of brethren'.[12] This form of confession of sins and declaration of forgiveness could be practiced between Christians, 'where two or three are gathered together' (as Luther added), and may be differentiated from the power of the keys in the more formal sense as administered by the clergy of the Church. The practice of mutual exhortation, confession, and consolation had something of a career in later Lutheran Pietism in the conventicles known as the *collegia pietatis*.[13] John Wesley learned the practice of group confession from the pietistic Moravian Brethren and included it as a part of the Methodist class meetings.[14]

For Pietism and Methodism, the confession of sins was the highest expression of Christian fellowship because it was a sharing in one another's conflicts and a mutual pursuit of holiness. For Luther, *the confession of sins was a way of living out one's baptism*—a putting to death of the old Adam so that the new person could arise, cleansed and righteous, to serve God and neighbour. Because the Christian life was a daily struggle between the old life and the new, many forms of absolution were needed to empower the Christian to live the new life in Christ. Among these Luther valued highly private confession, which he sometimes called 'the sacrament of absolution'.

2. PRIVATE CONFESSION IN THE REFORMATION CHURCHES

(a) In the Lutheran Church Orders

Luther's influence was strong on the Church orders which regulated ecclesiastical polity and discipline and liturgical practice in the territorial churches which embraced the Reformation. Many of the sixteenth century Church orders provided for private confession.[15] But the fate of private confession in the Lutheran Churches is tied to the *examination for Holy Communion* which Luther also introduced in his *Formula Missae et Communionis* of 1523.[16] Those who desired to receive Holy Communion were to announce their intention to the pastor, who was then to examine the communicants about what the Lord's Supper is, what its benefits are, and what they expect to receive from it. Communicants should be able to recite the Words of Institution from memory. For more learned people, this catechetical examination might be given only once in a lifetime. For most communicants it was administered at least once annually. But it could also include private confession and absolution, which Luther continued to regard as a fitting preparation for Holy Communion. Unfortunately, the terms 'examination' and 'confession' sometimes included each other. This *conflation of examination and confession* is witnessed to in the *Augsburg Confession*, Art. XXV: 'Confession has not been abolished in our churches, for it is not customary to administer the body of Christ except to those who have previously been examined and absolved.'[17] As Peter Brunner points out, the free element—private confession—was linked with the obligatory element—catechetical examination.[18] Moreover, the pastor had to use his judgment to discern who would be required to undergo this examination and who could be excused from it. The danger was great that the educated and noble classes would be excused from both the examination and the confession, although private confession always remained theoretically an independent means of grace. With the demise of the catechetical examination during the eighteenth century, all that was left for communion preparation was the *general confession*.

(b) In the Theology of John Calvin (1509–1564)

Private confession was *quickly abandoned in the Reformed Churches*, although we shall see that they developed an interest in public confession associated with ecclesiastical discipline. Nevertheless, John Calvin, while rejecting penance as a sacrament, came to *value a non-obligatory use of private confession*. Changes in his discussion of the confession of sins in the *Institutes of the Christian Religion* (1536) came after his experience as a pastor in Strassbourg, where he was influenced by Martin Bucer at a time when Bucer was in conversation with Luther. Calvin maintained that the power of the keys is exercised in the preaching of the Gospel and that baptism is the sacrament of forgiveness. But he recognised confession to God alone, to a brother in the form of mutual consolation, and to a brother against whom one has offended in an act of reconciliation. In the 1539 edition of the *Institutes* he added to the second form of confession that pastors are the most suitable persons to whom to make confession and from whom to receive absolution.[19] In the 1560 edition of the *Institutes* he went further and identified with pastors the authority to remit sins and loose souls (Matt. 16:19; 18:18; John 20:23) because they are 'constituted by God witnesses and as it were sureties, to certify our consciences of the remission of sins'.[20] To prevent a return to an *opus operatum* view of absolution, however, Calvin advised that *absolution be followed by spiritual direction*. Absolution does not take effect automatically;

it must be received in faith. Pastors were to help troubled sinners come to an assurance of forgiveness.

In spite of Calvin's teaching, private confession has had *virtually no career in the Reformed Churches*. Calvin was a second-generation reformer, and Reformed practices were well established before Calvin came along. His theology was widely embraced, but not all his ritual proposals.

(c) In the Anglican Books of Common Prayer

The eucharistic liturgy of the Prayer Book of King Edward VI (1549) contained an apologia for non-compulsory private confession for those 'whose conscience is troubled and greued in any thing'.[21] Although this exhortation was revised in the 1552 Prayer Book, the principle of non-compulsory private confession was maintained and was specifically provided for as a part of the ministry to the sick.[22] Nevertheless, *private confession waned in the Church of England* and among the Puritans it was eschewed for fear of a reversion to priestly authority over Christians.

3. CONFESSION OF SINS IN THE LITURGY

While private confession fell out of use in the Reformation Churches, the *confession of sins in liturgical orders was augmented*. The reformers understood the Gospel to be the forgiveness of the sinner for Christ's sake, and believed that the principal benefit of Holy Communion is forgiveness. Preparation for Holy Communion therefore rightfully entailed confession of sins. Prayers of confession in Reformation liturgies became statements of the sinful human condition and the need for forgiveness. Such a confession had, as its response, a general declaration of grace or an actual pronouncement of forgiveness.

Luther did not provide for confession and absolution in either his Latin or German orders of mass; nor did Ulrich Zwingli in his Latin or German Communion Services. However, Zwingli's 1525 Liturgy of the Word was based on the medieval Office of Prone (a pulpit office) in which the sermon concluded with a general confession of sins.[23] Some of the conservative Lutheran church orders, such as Brandenburg-Nürnberg 1533 and Mark Brandenburg 1540, retained the preparatory prayer for the priest known as the *Confiteor*, only omitting all references to intercessions by the Virgin Mary and the saints.[24] It was in the German liturgies of Strassbourg, beginning with the order of Mass prepared by Diebold Schwarz in 1524, that the *confiteor* was *rewritten into a general confession of sins intending to include the whole congregation*.[25] The Swedish Mass of Olavus Petri (1531) also began with an original prayer of confession followed by a prayer for forgiveness said by the priest 'over the people'.[26]

In 1524, the year Schwarz published his German Mass, Martin Bucer published *Grund und Ursach*, in which he laid the *groundwork for further liturgical reform*. He indicated that when the congregation comes together on Sunday, the minister admonishes them to make confession of their sins and pray for pardon: then he confesses to God on behalf of the whole congregation, prays for pardon, and declares the remission of sins to those who believe.[27] *Forms of confession of sins were developed in successive revisions of the Strassbourg liturgy*; the 1539 *Psalter mit aller Kirchenübung* provides three forms of confession. The third is a long prayer which goes through the ten commandments. The second was composed by Bucer and was adopted by Calvin for his French liturgy of 1540. He also took over from the German liturgy the comfortable words and the absolution. These were dropped from his Geneva liturgy of 1542; the absolution was replaced with a prayer for pardon. In his Strassbourg liturgy Calvin had the congregation sing a metrical version of the Decalogue after the absolution; this was replaced in Geneva with a metrical psalm. John Knox, who was ministering to British exiles in Geneva during the reign of Queen Mary (1553–1558), took over Calvin's *La Forme des Prières* into his English service book, *The Forme of Prayers*, which became the basis of the *Book of Common Order* of the Church of Scotland—including Calvin's prayers of confession and for pardon.[28]

The English reformers derived prayers of confession and absolution from continental Reformation sources, but placed them in a *different position within the eucharistic liturgy*. The 1548 Order of Communion included a general confession and absolution based on archbishop Hermann's *Consultation* (the Cologne Church Order of 1543). These materials were included in the 1549 Prayer Book. The confession of sins, absolution, and comfortable words were placed just prior to the ministration of Holy Communion—an arrangement that had a precedent in medieval orders for receiving Holy Communion outside of Mass. In the 1552 Prayer Book, the confession, absolution, and comfortable words were relocated to a place in the offertory-section of the liturgy, after the prayer 'for the whole state of Christes Church militant here in earth' and the exhortation to communion—an arrangement that could appeal to the medieval Office of Prone. The orders for Morning and Evening Prayer in the 1552 Prayer Book began with confession and absolution, the texts of which are a masterful expression of the Reformation doctrines of sin and forgiveness—sin as an offence against God and forgiveness by God to those who repent for Christ's sake.[29]

(a) The Lutheran Beichtgottesdienst

While the Anglican prayer offices began with a penitential rite, *Lutheran Saturday Vespers acquired a penitential character.*[30] The Cologne Church Order provides a typical example.[31] Those who had announced their intention to receive communion at the Sunday service attended Vespers on the evening before the Lord's Supper was celebrated. This office included psalmody sung by the clergy and choir boys, antiphon and responsory, a hymn, the Magnificat, and collects. Then the congregation sang a German psalm and the pastor read from I Cor. 11 and John 6, after which he gave an exposition on the sacrament and an exhortation to the communicants. This was followed by the examination of the communicants and confession with absolution. When the number of communicants became large (and pastors were always exhorting their people to receive the sacrament more frequently), the examination and confession became a mere formality and absolution was given to several penitents at once. From this it was a short step to *replacing private confession with a general confession.* Other factors which contributed to the demise of private confession included the revolt against the offering of the *Beichtpfennig* to the priest, and the Pietist dislike of the unconditional absolution. Under Reformed influence, Pietists felt that spiritual direction should be provided and this could not be done within the formal confines of either private confession or the confessional service.

(b) The Anglican Commination Office

A penitential service was included in the 1549 *Book of Common Prayer* to replace the Ash Wednesday liturgy in the Sarum Use, and it was retained in subsequent Prayer Books. An initial exhortation reminded the congregation of the public discipline of the early Church and expressed a hope for its restoration. After 'sentences of God cursing' are read to instill 'earnest and true repentance', there followed a homily proclaiming forgiveness of sins, Psalm 51, the Kyrie, the Lord's Prayer, two prayers, and an anthem which in the Sarum Use had been associated with the imposition of ashes.[32]

5. PUBLIC CONFESSION

The Anglican Commination Office shows the influence of archbishop Hermann's *Consultation* which, in a section on The Ban, includes a discussion of conversion and true penitence. Martin Bucer, a principal author of the

Cologne Church Order, had developed a concern for *Church discipline* in reaction to the Anabaptist witness that the Church must be reformed in life and conduct as well as in doctrine and cult. The Anabaptist Schleitheim Confession (1527), Art. II, identified the Ban (excommunication) as the means of keeping the Church pure. Bucer, too, taught that *communio* requires *disciplina*, that if the Church is to be a *Leibensgemeinschaft* (a community of love) it must be a *Zuchtgemeinschaft* (a community of discipline).[33]

Bucer envisioned a structure of Church discipline based on Matt. 18:15–18, in which notorious sinners would be censured by the pastor and elders of the Church and excommunicated if they failed to confess their sins and express repentance. He was never able to implement this practice in Strassbourg, where the magistrates were apprehensive of too independent a position for the Church. He was able to introduce censure and excommunication in Hesse in 1537, in which the accused had the right of appeal to the congregation or to the synod. Bucer also realised his vision in the Kassel and Cologne Church Orders, and Calvin carried this practice to Geneva where excommunication was enforced by the civil magistrates. Knox also brought it to Scotland, where the censure, punishment, confession, absolution, and reconciliation of penitents was practiced in the Kirk for two hundred years after the Reformation.[34] Similar procedures were used by the Puritans in New England.[35] The Swedish Church Order of archbishop Laurentius Petri (1571) also provided for excommunication. Its provision that those under discipline should leave the service after the sermon revived the ancient distinction between the liturgy of the catechumens and the liturgy of the faithful.[36] Public penance survived in Sweden into the nineteenth century.

Provision for excommunication and public confession and absolution in the various Reformation Church orders testify to the concern for maintaining *authentic Christian community*. The problem is that Church discipline worked only where Church and State were in close partnership. This created a correlation between being a good citizen and being a faithful communicant which could only undermine the vocation of the Church to be an eschatological community.

6. REVIVAL OF PRIVATE CONFESSION IN THE NINETEENTH CENTURY

(a) In the Oxford Movement

One of the concerns of the leaders of the Oxford Movement, especially John Keble (1792–1866) and Edward Bouverie Pusey (1800–1882), was for *holiness of life cultivated within the worshipping community* of the Church.[37] They found provision for private confession, with its possibilities for 'spiritual direction', implicit within the Anglican Prayer Book, and worked to implement it on a voluntary basis. Both Keble and Pusey preached sermons and wrote tracts on 'auricular confession', and declared it to be of great value to the sin-sick soul. They also issued several manuals for the guidance of confessors and penitants. In these they followed the Roman Catholic view which regarded private confession as a valuable preparation for Holy Communion.

(b) In Neuendettelsau under Wilhelm Löhe (1808–1872)

Contemporary with the English Tractarians, Wilhelm Löhe, pastor of the small Bavarian town of Neuendettelsau, was *rediscovering private confession as the appropriate pastoral tool for the care of souls.*[38] He defined *Beichte* on the basis of Luther's Catechisms as confession and absolution. Knowledge of sin comes from the law of God; and only self-examination in the light of God's law can produce the true repentance which should accompany confession. He also distinguished three kinds of confession: before God, to the neighbour, and to the *Beichtvater*. He does not argue that this last confession is commanded by God; but absolution is commanded by God, and there should be no absolution without confession. Such a confession was a living out of baptism. However, in his consideration of the power of the keys, Löhe also concluded that confession and absolution is only a half measure it if is not joined with the power to retain sins (refuse absolution) and to deny the Lord's Supper.

According to Gerhard Ottersberg, Löhe preached for years about the value of private confession before he invited people to come.[39] When they came he encouraged them to speak from the heart rather than to use set forms. The deaconess community, which Löhe founded in Neuendettelsau, also adopted this practice. When people came to announce for Holy Communion, either Pastor Löhe himself or the deacons asked a person to step aside if there was cause. These persons were then privately admonished and admitted to Holy Communion on confession. Those who were unrepentant were denied admission. This practice was questioned by the Church authorities but not forbidden. Löhe also encouraged individuals to admonish one another whenever sin occurred, and this was practiced in the deaconess community and the mission school.

7. THE CONFESSION OF SINS TODAY IN THE REFORMATION CHURCHES

We have seen a *variety of forms of confession of sins in the Reformation Churches. Secret confession* by the individual to God alone of either specific sins or of one's sinful state in general has always beem emphasised in Protestant preaching and teaching. But, as Dietrich Bonhoeffer observed, if this secret confession is the only practice of the invididual, one may miss the 'breakthrough to certainty' of forgiveness which takes place in confession before an absolution from a confessor.[40]

General confession is provided in most Protestant liturgies, followed by a declaration of grace or a prayer of absolution. This is usually placed at the beginning of the liturgy, although sometimes it follows the sermon or is included in the intercessions following the model of the medieval Prone. Among Lutherans, *announcing for communion* is no longer widely practiced, nor is the confessional service often used. Nevertheless, *services of corporate confession* with individual absolution and the laying on of hands remain in worship books and agendas.[41]

Public discipline is seldom practiced today; but it is provided for in congregational and judicatory constitutions. Pastors work to achieve reconciliatory confession where one person has sinned against another. The 'mutual conversation and consolation of brethren' is practiced in small groups and in pastoral care.

Private or individual confession is not widespread in Protestant churches, but it is practised, especially in Anglican and Lutheran circles. It received a renewal in the practice of the Confessing Church in Germany during the Nazi era[42] and in the Protestant monastery at Taizé, France.[43] The use of individual confession before a confessor with sacramental absolution has been advocated as a spiritual discipline[44] and as a tool in pastoral care.[45] A form is provided in the 1978 *Lutheran Book of Worship*.[46]

Notes

1. On the history of indulgences, see B. Poschmann *Penance and the Anointing of the Sick* tr. F. Courtney (Freiburg 1968) pp. 210ff.

2. On the indulgence controversy, see E. Iserloh, J. Glazik and H. Jedin *Reformation and Counter Reformation* (*History of the Church*, edited by Hubert Jedin and John Dolan, V) (New York 1980) pp. 42–51.

3. See *Martin Luthers Werke* (Kritische Gesamtausgabe, Weimar 1883ff.) (hereafter referred to as *WA*) 1 pp. 63–65, 94–99, 138–141.

4. *WA* 1 pp. 31–38.

5. See *Resolutiones disputationum de indulgentiarum virtute* (1518) *WA* 1 pp. 526–628; *Sermo de poenitentia* (1518) *WA* 1 pp. 319–324; *Ein Sermon von dem Sakrament der Busse* (1519) *WA* 2 pp. 714–723; *De captivitate babylonica* (1520) *WA* 6 pp. 543–549.

6. *WA* 10/III p. 64.

7. *Der Grosser Katechismus* 'Ein kurze Vermehung zu der Beicht'; *Die Bekenntnisschriften der evangelisch-lutherischen Kirche* (Göttingen 1930) (hereafter referred to as *Bek.*) pp. 725ff.

8. *Der Kleine Katechismus* 'Wie man die Einfältigen soll lehren beichten' *Bek.* pp. 517f.

9. B. Werkström *Bekännelse och Avlösning: En typologisk undersökning av Luthers, Thurneysens och Buchmans biktuppfattningar* (Studia Theologica Lundensia 24) (Lund 1963) pp. 32ff.

10. Duns Scotus and William of Occam held that the essence of penance lies in absolution and that contrition, confession, and satisfaction are necessary as a disposition to receive the sacrament: see Poschmann, the work cited in note 1, pp. 184ff.

11. *Kl. Kat.*, VI; *Bek.* p. 520.

12. *S.A.*, Pars III, Art. IV; *Bek.* p. 449.

13. See *Philipp Jakob Speners Pia Desideria* ed. K. Aland (Kleine Texte für Vorlesungen und Übungen 170, Berlin 1940 and 1952) proposals II and V

14. See T. Dearing *Wesleyan and Tractarian Worship* (London 1966) pp. 62ff.

15. See L. Klein *Evangelisch-Lutherische Beichte: Lehre und Praxis* (Paderborn 1961) pp. 174ff.

16. *WA* 12 p. 215f.

17. *A.C.* XXV, 1; *Bek.* p. 97.

18. P. Brunner *Zur Lehre vom Gottesdienst der im Namen Jesu versammelten Gemeinde* (Leitourgia; Handbuch des evangelischen Gottesdienst I), (Kassel 1954) p. 338.

19. Jean Calvin. *Institution de la religion chrétienne* (ed. Belles-Lettres) II 200. See M. Thurian *La Confession* (Neuchâtel 1953) ch. 1.

20. Jean Calvin *Institution de la religion chrétienne* III ch. IV, par. 12; ed. La Société Calviniste de France, Genève 1857, III, pp. 109–110.

21. *The First and Second Prayer Books of King Edward VI* (Everyman's Library No. 448) (London and New York 1910) p. 217.

22. *Ibid.* pp.262, 419.

23. See B. Thompson *Liturgies of the Western Church* (Cleveland 1961), p. 148.

24. *Die evangelischen Kirchenordnungen des XVI. Jahrhunderts*, ed. E. Sehling (Leipzig 1902ff.) XI p. 188; III pp. 67f.

25. See W. Maxwell *An Outline of Christian Worship* (London 1936) pp. 91f.

26. See E. Yelverton *The Mass in Sweden. Its Development from the Latin Rite from 1531 to 1917* (Henry Bradshaw Society LVII) (London 1920) pp. 32–34.

27. See Thompson, the work cited in note 23, p. 161.

28. See W. Maxwell *John Knox's Genevan Service Book*, 1556 (Edinburgh 1931).

29. *The First and Second Prayer Books*, cited in note 21, pp. 347–349.

30. See Klein, the work cited in note 15, pp. 185ff.

31. See G. J. van de Pol *Martin Bucer's Liturgical Ideas* (Assen 1954) pp. 138ff.

32. *The First and Second Prayer Books*, the work cited in note 21, pp. 280ff., 430ff.

33. Van de Pol, the work cited in note 31, pp. 62ff.

34. See W. Maxwell *A History of Worship in the Church of Scotland* (London, Glasgow and New York 1955) pp. 145–155.

35. See D. Adams *Meeting House to Camp Meeting. Toward a History of American Free Church Worship from 1620 to 1835* (Austin and Saratoga 1981) pp. 50–55.

36. See Y. Brilioth *Eucharistic Faith and Practice, Evangelical and Catholic* tr. A. G. Hebert (London 1965) p. 253.

37. See Dearing, the work cited in note 14, pp. 66–70.

38. See K. Korby *Löhe Theology of Pastoral Care* (Th. D. Thesis, Concordia Seminary in Exile, St Louis 1976) pp. 111ff., 188ff.

39. Gerhard Ottersberg 'Wilhelm Loehe' *Lutheran Quarterly* IV (1952) 180–181.

40. Dietrich Bonhoeffer *Life Together* (New York 1954) pp. 115–118.

41. See 'Corporate Confession and Forgiveness' *Lutheran Book of Worship* (Minneapolis and Philadelphia 1978) pp. 193–195.

42. See Bonhoeffer, the work cited in note 40, pp. 110ff. This book grew out of Bonhoeffer's experience in the 'underground' seminary of the Confessing Church.

43. See M. Thurian *La Confession*, cited in note 19.

44. See M. Marty *The Hidden Discipline* (St Louis 1962) pp. 95–101.

45. See E. Thurneysen *Die Lehre von der Seelsorge* (Zürich 1946).

46. 'Individual Confession and Forgiveness' *Lutheran Book of Worship* pp. 196–197.

Geoffrey Wainwright

Confession of Fault and Reconciliation between the Churches

1. FIRST FORMULATIONS

In an article written before Vatican II and entitled 'Forgotten truths concerning the sacrament of penance', Karl Rahner[1] brought back to light the fact that an individual Christian, in sinning, *sins against the Church*:

> The Christian who is baptized meets the holy God of grace as a member of the Church. ... The holiness of the Church (her Spirit) is given to the Christian as his own, because he is her member—and he is to give his holiness (his life in the Spirit) to the Church, so that she will be the holy one. The Christian who sins offends, therefore, against his own attachment to the Church (which is essential to him as a Christian) and against the Church herself. ... He renders the Church herself sinful in a certain regard.

If an individual Christian may thus sin against the holiness of the Church, so may individual Christians, by their features in truth and love (*alêtheountes en agapêi*. ... Eph. 4:15), sin against the unity of the Church. When faced by the 'evil mystery' of collective or corporate division among Christians, one may (I suggest) raise the further question: Can an 'ecclesial community' (either in the sense of a particular, local church, or in the sense of a confessional tradition) sin against '*the* Church as such', that is to say, against 'the Church catholic' (either in the sense of 'the Church universal', or in the sense of 'the one true

Church of Jesus Christ')? The answer one gives to this question will govern the sense in which CONFESSION OF FAULT will play a part in an eventual reconciliation of divided Christendom.

Let us look at a second, related question. Can schism only *separate* schismatic individuals and groups *from* the Church? Or may schism rather take place and persist in some way *within* the Church? In the first case, there could only be an 'ecumenism of return', a reconciliation that *brought back* the schismatics to the one, 'uninterrupted' Church. If, however, schism could somehow be located *inside* the Church, then the healing would be an *internal* process. The answer given to this question will govern the sense in which RECONCILIATION is understood and celebrated in an eventual restoration of Christian unity.

It is evident that *entire ecclesiologies are at stake* in these two questions. Concretely, the Orthodox especially cannot conceive a 'sinning' and 'divisible' Church. On the other hand, Protestants refuse to give the Church an independent hypostatic existence apart from the *simul iusti et peccatores* who compose it—and they would therefore be surprised if sin did not manifest itself in visible disunity among Christians. Let us see if contemporary Roman Catholicism has any help to offer in reflection on the two questions just outlined.

2. ROMAN INDICATIONS

On 29 September 1963, at the opening of the second session of Vatican II, Pope Paul VI addressed these words to the observers from 'the Christian denominations separated from the Catholic Church':

> If we are in any way to blame for this separation, we humbly beg God's forgiveness. And we ask our brothers' pardon for any injuries they feel they have sustained from us. For our part, we willingly forgive whatever injuries the Catholic Church has suffered, and forget the grief she has endured as a result of the long years of dissension and separation. May the heavenly Father deign to hear our prayers and grant us true brotherly peace.

Did the 'we' mean simply the pope, personally? Probably not simply so, although it is probable that, given the exquisite conscience and sensibility of Paul VI, he felt some individual responsibility. Did the pope, then, mean by 'we' an aggregation of Roman Catholics, collectively? Or is it even possible that the pope was speaking for the Roman Catholic Church as such, corporately? In December 1975, on the tenth anniversary of the mutual lifting of the 'sentences of excommunication' between Rome and Constantinople, Pope Paul knelt before Metropolitan Meliton, the emissary of the Ecumenical Patriarch, and kissed his feet. What a gesture, considering how long such obeisance (*proskynesis*) had been an ecclesiologically significant claim of the papacy![2]

On his visit to the land of Luther in 1980, Pope John Paul II said of the history of division:

> 'We will not pass judgment on one another' (Rom. 14:13). But let us mutually confess our guilt. With respect to the grace of unity also, it is a fact that 'all have sinned' (Rom. 3:23). We must recognise and acknowledge that fact in all seriousness and draw the appropriate conclusions. ... If we do not try to avoid the facts, we realise that human failings are to blame for the harmful division of Christians, and that our own refusals have time and again hindered the steps that are possible and necessary to unity.[3]

Turning back from the popes to the Council, we must look at the 'Catholic principles of ecumenism' set forth in the decree *Unitatis redintegratio*.[4] From paragraph 3 it is clear that the Roman Catholic Church has made *baptism*, and the faith in Christ which baptism signifies, the ground of its participation in the ecumenical movement. That is an important step. Cyprian had considered void any 'baptisms' performed outside the Catholic Church. Augustine ruled that baptisms received at the hands of Donatists should not be repeated, but their efficacy began only when a schismatic was reconciled to the Catholic Church. The Council of Trent recognised baptism by heretics as 'true baptism' provided it was administered under invocation of the Trinity and with the intention of doing what the Church does (Denz. 1617).

The earliest generous interpretations of that principle were probably governed more by pastoral concern for the salvation of individuals than by the discernment of ecclesial values outside the Roman Catholic fold. *Vatican II is much more positive*. The decree on ecumenism recognises that important elements of ecclesial life 'can exist outside the visible boundaries of the Catholic Church' (*UR* 3). 'Coming from Christ and leading back to him', these elements 'belong by right to the one Church of Christ' (*ibid.*). The same decree appears, moreover, to take the idea of 'vestigia Ecclesiae' further than it had been taken in the earlier days of modern Roman Catholic ecumenism: it declares that 'the separated churches and communities as such ... have been by no means deprived of significance and importance in the mystery of salvation' (*ibid.*). When the text immediately goes to say that 'the Spirit of Christ has not refrained from using them as means of salvation which derive their efficacy from the very fulness of grace and truth entrusted to the Catholic

Church', the precise status of other 'churches and communities' has to be interpreted in light of the famous and difficult statement of *Lumen gentium* that 'the sole Church of Christ ... *subsists in* the Catholic Church, which is governed by the successor of Peter and by the bishops in communion with him' (*LG* 8).

The next most important statement of *Unitatis redintegratio* for our question was that those baptised in other communities 'are put in some, though imperfect, communion with the Catholic Church' (*UR* 3). The clear implication is that the future reconciliation of Christendom will be a 'family reunion'; it will be, in some sense, *internal to the Church*. A further hint in the same direction—although the dominant motive may for the moment still be pastoral rather than strictly ecclesiological—is the admission of other Christians, in rare and urgent circumstances, to eucharistic communion in the Roman Catholic Church. As yet, Roman Catholics are not permitted, by their own discipline, to receive communion elsewhere, except that Vatican II sought that exceptional hospitality from the Eastern Orthodox Churches (although, as far as I know, only the Moscow Patriarchate has accorded it). It thus appears likely that Roman Catholic recognition of ordained ministries in other churches or communities will remain an indispensable part of the achievement of complete ecclesial communion.

3. SYSTEMATIC REFLECTIONS

In the aforementioned article Karl Rahner writes thus on the relation between *baptism and the serious ecclesiastical penance* ('paenitentia secunda') of the patristic period:

> Baptism is forgiveness by free favour, a new creation, simply remission, sheer direct action of the blood of Christ. Penance, even as a sacrament, is laborious atonement, baptism in one's own tears, not a rebirth of a sudden kind, but a slow bitter cure by one's own efforts, even though these must be supported by the grace of God.[5]

Yet, despite this difference, baptism remains, as M. F. Mannion has lately argued, the 'systemic foundation', even for the more recent and milder 'penance of devotion'.[6]

It seems to me that the ancient relation between baptism and the reconciliation of the erring and repentant Christian to the Church provides a valuable perspective for the *reconciliation also of the churches*. *Four steps* may be envisaged in this process. It will be important, first, to maximise the recognition of 'the one baptism' which, for example, the Lima text of Faith and Order sees as existing in common among the divided churches.[7] This must not be too easily presupposed, since the churches need to agree explicitly on the essential meaning and effect of baptism (the Lima text is a contribution towards that) and also on the broader dogmatic context in which baptism is understood and performed (here the World Council of Churches study 'Towards the Common Expression of the Apostolic Faith Today' is added to the efforts of many bilateral dialogues). What seems clear is that the course of Christian history has rendered a strictly Cyprianic (and perhaps even Augustinian) ecclesiology and sacramentology untenable: in one way or another, *all churches appear to recognise the presence of baptism and the Christian faith outside their own institutional boundaries.* Wherever baptism and faith are found, they occur by sheer grace. They, and it, are fundamental to all Christian and ecclesial unity.

As the next step, the *gravity of disunity* must be recognised: it is an offence against the grace of the Gospel signified in baptism. Failures in truth and love must be repented of. The sin that characterises the origin and persistence of division must be confessed. Vatican II declared:

> In this one and only Church of God from its beginnings there arose certain rifts, which the Apostle strongly censures as damnable. But in subsequent centuries much more serious dissensions appeared, and large communities became separated from full communion with the Catholic Church—for which, often enough, men of both sides were to blame. (*UR* 3)

In their 'common declaration' of 7 December 1965,[8] Pope Paul VI and Patriarch Athenagoras I expressed 'regret for historical errors':

> They regret the offensive words, the reproaches without foundation and the reprehensible gestures which on both sides marked or accompanied the sad events of that period [i.e. 1054]. ... They deplore the troublesome precedents and the later events which, under the influence of various factors, among them lack of understanding and mutual hositility, eventually led to the effective rupture of ecclesiastical communion.

Such testimonies are perhaps sufficient to justify Karl Rahner's ecclesiological concept of a 'Church of sinners' (*Kirche der Sünder*).[9] That expression appears to move beyond the Eastern Orthodox reluctance to say more than that there are 'sinners in the Church'—and yet stops short of Protestant talk of a 'sinful Church'.

The third step will be the *act of reconciliation itself*. If our model is the patristic reconciliation of the penitent individual to ecclesial communion, then in our ecumenical adaptation the delicate question arises: *who* is to reconcile *whom* 'to the Church'? Since the confession of 'fraternal offence' (see Matt. 5:23–24) will presumably have been mutual, it will be appropriate, in the first place, that each church or community expresses *its* pardon of the others. But who, next, is to beseech, declare or enact *God's* pardon—and thus establish reconciliation 'to *the* Church as such'? Or should one perhaps rather speak of 'the reconciliation *of* the Church'? For who, in a divided Christendom, can with full authenticity pronounce forgiveness 'in the name of *the* Church'? If Protestants were willing to hear God's forgiveness declared to them by the Orthodox and the Roman Catholic Churches (Orthodox/Catholic reconciliation itself belonging *ex hypothesi* to the process!), the Orthodox and the Catholics would be bearing witness to the important values contained in their traditional insistence upon the indivisibility of the visible Church, while Protestants would be recognising the inadequacy of their tendency either (in classical Protestantism) to take refuge in the invisibility of the true Church or (in liberal Protestantism) to acquiesce in ecclesial divisions under the guise of 'pluralism'. I will leave it to Catholics and Orthodox to determine what benefit each might derive from hearing God's forgiveness declared by the other—and perhaps even by a Protestant.

The fourth step will consist in *enjoying the fruits of repentance, forgiveness and reconciliation in a shared eucharistic communion.* This will seal and manifest the blessings brought by the completed penitential process to the churches and the Church. According to the Roman *Ordo Paenitentiae* of 1973, penance is a 'liturgy by which the Church continually renews itself' (§ 11). If that is already true for the ordinary practice of individual penance, how much more may we expect from the communal reconciliation of the churches in the Church! Moreover, it is not only a matter of the renewal of the Church's internal life: the Church should also, as a result of ecumenical reconciliation, be able to accomplish more authentically its external mission. 'In a broken world,' as the Lima text puts it, the Church has a ministry of reconciliation.[10] Pope John Paul II, in *Reconciliatio et Paenitentia* (1984), reaffirmed the importance of this aspect of 'the mission of the Church today'. According to St Augustine, Christians have been initiated into 'a reconciled world'.[11] Having accepted God's reconciliation (2 Cor. 5:19), the Church itself becomes a kind of sacrament, i.e. sign and instrument, of reconciliation in the world. With the cessation of the counter-testimony presented by Christian disunity, the Church will present a more credible witness to the Gospel of a divine reconciliation which implies a reconciliation among humankind. Jesus prayed for the unity of his disciples, so that the world might believe in his own divine mission (John 17:21).

4. LITURGICAL SUGGESTIONS

Relying on the classic liturgical study of Jungmann,[12] Karl Rahner gives the following 'theological' description of the *patristic liturgy of penance:*

> A staggering liturgy this, the liturgy of the Church of sinners, the solemnly regulated appearance of the Church of sinners before the seat of grace of the Father who holds the Cross of the Son; the liturgy of the prodigal son which consists in man's confessing himself before the holy God to be what he is of himself, namely a sinner; the sacrifice of praise by the lips which God himself must open. ... The early Church celebrated this terrible and healing liturgy of the Church of sinners most 'solemnly' (if we may say so) in her penitential discipline. The 'celebrant' of this liturgy [Rahner has already given grounds for calling the confessing sinner a 'celebrant'] wore a special vestment for this, viz. the penitential robe; he fasted and wept; over and over again during the long period of penance he let the representative of Christ impose hands upon him, in prayer and in exorcism of the powers of darkness; the whole congregation celebrated with him, praying and interceding on his behalf. This liturgy took place in the presence of the whole saintly congregation; the distance from the pure bliss of the Altar, which was both punishment and healing, was clearly brought out. The priest (bishop) took part in the prayer and fasting. He made his grace-giving word of forgiveness still more tangible and clear by his imposition of the hand. ...[13]

How might that early liturgy of individual penance and reconciliation be *adapted for our present ecumenical purpose?*

From the international joint commission between Catholics and Lutherans we may draw the suggestion that ecumenical reconciliation needs to find expression in liturgical celebrations that include 'both penitence and thanksgiving' (*sowohl Busse wie Danksagung*).[14] Remembering the essential character of Christian worship as Word and Sacrament, we might envisage, for a constitutive service of reconciliation between churches, a liturgical order with the following principal points:

i. Appropriate introit-psalms would be Psalms 122 and 133 (Hebrew numbering).

ii. The opening prayer might be borrowed from the prayer before communion in the Roman Mass: 'Domine Jesu Christe, qui dixisti apostolis tuis ...' The problematic of Christian and ecclesial existence—between the sad history of disunity, on the one hand, and the fundamental faith and eschatological nature of the Church, on the other—is reflected in the tension, even the ambiguity, of the petition: 'Look not on our sins, but on the faith of your Church'. The gift of ecclesial peace and unity (*pacificare et coadunare*) can only be prayed for.

iii.   A suitable Epistle and Gospel would be Eph. 4:1–16 and John 17. These should be expounded in a homily.

iv.   The response would come in the recitation of the creed. The character of this act as an 'anamnesis' of baptism—the common baptism on the basis of which the reconciliation is taking place—could be enhanced if, as in the renewal of baptismal vows at the Paschal Vigil, the confession of faith took the form of questions and answers.

v.   It is upon this baptismal foundation that the 'reconciliation of penitents' would then take place. First, representatives of each community would confess before the other communities, perhaps in words adapted from the penitential beginning of the Mass: 'I confess to almighty God, and to you, my brothers and sisters. ...' Each time, the respective confessing community would hear from the other communities the assurance that—at least at the level of Christian brotherhood and sisterhood—their confession had been heard and their forgiveness granted. After this *mutual* confession and pardon, all the communities together would then make a *common* prayer of confession to God. The linguistic form would be that of the first person plural, as in the 'general confessions' of the Anglican liturgy: 'Almighty and most merciful God, we have erred and strayed from thy ways. ...' This would be at least a collective admission of guilt; it might even be a strictly corporate confession, if it followed a hint in the current liturgy of the United Methodist Church: '... we have failed to be an obedient Church'. The question of who would pronounce the absolution has already been raised earlier: perhaps the best solution, as we shall see, is to pass immediately into the 'prayers of the people'.

vi.   The prayers of the people could embrace three themes. First place would be occupied, in fact, by *supplications* for the divine forgiveness. There is ancient support for the 'absolution' taking this rhetorical form. Jungmann makes clear, from the Gelasian sacramentary, that the oldest material and 'firm kernel' (*fester Kern*) of the reconciliation of penitents included three such *prayers* said by the bishop: 'The bishop pronounced the reconciliation in deprecative form, or more accurately in supplicative form, in the form namely of the so-called *supplicationes*; these were orations in the ordinary style of the Roman oration, containing the petition directed to God (the *supplicatio*), that he forgive the sinner'.[15] Second would come prayers for the internal renewal of the Church and for the more authentic prosecution of its evangelical mission of reconciliation in the world. The relation between these first two parts of the 'common prayers' might be seen in the perspective of the Catholic/Lutheran commission: 'In the act of penance and reconciliation ... our churches turn resolutely to the future and leave to God the judgment upon the past'.[16] The third theme in the prayers would retrieve the positive elements in the past by a commemoration of significant figures in our common—and *divided*—histories, in such a way that even controversial characters became 'transfigured' in an authentic 'communion of the saints' where their virtues were honoured and their failings forgotten.

vii. The kiss of peace would complete the reconciliation of the communities among themselves and their common reconciliation to God.

viii. The achieved reconciliation would be enjoyed in a concelebrated eucharist. We have already mentioned the delicate question of recognition of ordained ministries. Let me suggest that at least one constitutive element in the reconciliation of ministries would be this concelebration of a eucharist—preferably 'in coena Domini', thereby recalling Christ's own institution and gift of the sacrament and ministry.

ix. The most appropriate occasion for this entire service of 'penitence and thanksgiving' by which the churches are to be reconciled would accordingly be Maundy Thursday, the Thursday in Holy Week. That is not only the day of the institution of the eucharist but also the day when, in the ancient Church, penitents were reconciled.

In case I have not already made enough 'impossible' suggestions, let me conclude by recalling, with Jungmann, that the period of proximate preparation for reconciliation was the season of Lent.[17] In the year appointed for ecumenical reconciliation among the churches, the churches could make their final spiritual preparations during the Lenten period. A sign of penitence would be abstention from celebrating the eucharist during those weeks—except on Sundays, when the advice once given by the abbé Paul Couturier on a particular occasion could be generalised:

> If you are a priest, I beg of you to offer the most holy Sacrifice on the coming feast of St. Bartholomew, 24 August, asking God's pardon for the acts of violence committed by our fathers, entreating him to change the atoning blood once shed into a spring of living waters wherein the Lamb-Redeemer will enable us to find once more our profound brotherhood in him.[18]

When the churches have been constitutively reconciled among themselves in a great general service of penitence and thanksgiving on Holy Thursday, the Christians in every locality will be able to celebrate a joyful Easter together three days later (provided the dispute concerning *that* date has also been settled ...).

Notes

1. K. Rahner *Theological Investigations* (London and Baltimore 1963) II 135–174, in particular 137 (*Schriften zur Theologie* Einsiedeln 1955 (1964[7]), II, 143–183, in particular p. 145).

2. H. Fries and K. Rahner *Einigung der Kirchen—reale Möglichkeit* (Quaestiones Disputatae 100) (Freiburg in Breisgau 1983) p. 82. Compare the Bull of Boniface VIII *Unam sanctam* (1302): 'It is altogether necessary to salvation for every human creature to be subject to the Roman pontiff' (Denz. 875).

3. *Papst Johannes Paulus II in Deutschland* (Verlautbarungen des Apostolischen Stuhls 25) (Bonn 1980) pp. 80 and 86.

4. English translations of Vatican II documents are taken from *Vatican Council II: The Conciliar and Post-Conciliar Documents* ed. A. Flannery (Dublin 1975).

5. K. Rahner *Theological Investigations* II p. 157 (German p. 166).

6. M. F. Mannon 'Penance and reconciliation: a systemic analysis' *Worship* 60 (1986) 98–118; see already Rahner, the work cited in note 1, pp. 173–174 (German p. 182).

7. *Baptism, Eucharist and Ministry* (Geneva 1982) 'Baptism' § 6 and commentary.

8. French text in AAS 58 (1966) 20–21.

9. See K. Rahner *Die Kirche der Sünder* (Freiburg in Breisgau 1948).

10. *Baptism, Eucharist and Ministry*, 'Ministry' § 1.

11. Augustine *Sermon* 96, 8 (PL 38, 588).

12. J. A. Jungmann *Die lateinischen Bussriten in ihrer geschichtlichen Entwicklung* (Innsbruck 1932). For a summary of the principal features, see J. A. Jungmann *The Early Liturgy to the time of Gregory the Great* (Notre Dame, Indiana 1959) pp. 240–248.

13. K. Rahner *Theological Investigations* II pp. 160–161 (German p. 169).

14. Gemeinsame römisch-katholische/evangelisch-lutherische Kommission *Einheit vor uns: Modelle, Formen und Phasen katholisch-lutherischer Kirchengemeinschaft* (Paderborn and Frankfurt 1985) § 69 (and see § 138).

15. J. A. Jungmann *The Early Liturgy* p. 244; for details see *Die lateinischen Bussriten* pp. 74–83, 238–242.

16. *Einheit vor uns,* § 139.

17. J. A. Jungmann *The Early Liturgy* pp. 245–246; details in *Die lateinischen Bussriten*, 44–74, where the author also treats 'the reception of heretics' as 'a kind of mitigated penance' ('eine Art gemildertes Bussverfahren', p. 60; and see 150).

18. M. Villain *L'Abbé Paul Couturier, apôtre de l'unité chrétienne* (Tournai 1957[2]) p. 208.

David Power

Editorial Conclusions

THE STARTING-POINT of this number of *Concilium* was the impression that the synod of bishops which discussed Penance and Reconciliation *had not adequately addressed the issues involved in the renewal of the sacrament of reconciliation* and the Church's penitential practice. From one point of view, the synodal documents concentrated too much on one element of the process of forgiveness and reconciliation, namely, the confession of sins to an ordained minister. From another point of view, it did not show much insight into the nature of the confession of sins as such and its overall place in the Christian life. The editors of *Concilium* decided to isolate this confession from the other acts of conversion, to see what problems arise from its misconception and misuse, to seek out its own inner intentionality and forms, and to discuss its appropriate place in contemporary Christian living.

The confession of sins as an act of the Christian person is clouded by current sacramental structures, its nature obscured by canonical obligations and by an excessive preoccupation with what has come to be known as the integrity of confession necessary to the reception of sacramental absolution. That it is more than a listing of sins and their submission, with a contrite heart, to judgment is made clear by some words of Pope Paul VI that have been integrated into the 1972 Order of Penance. Paul VI describes *metanoia* or conversion as a *profound change of the whole person* whereby one begins to consider, judge and arrange one's life according to the holiness and love of God.[1] This perception of one's life is mediated by an act of confession, made with a contrite heart and leading to acts of penance that serve to change the habits and outlook of one's life.

For Christians of the Western tradition, the model for confession is always in some sense the *Confessions* of Saint Augustine. In this work, one finds a profound attempt by the author to see his *life as a whole, both backwards and forwards*, to find in it the signs of sinfulness and aberration along with their causes, but more profoundly to unfold the continuing traces of God's grace and mercy. Acts are examined not simply in themselves, but in their motivations and in their relation to what Augustine became in performing them. They are placed in the setting of the person's ineradicable desire for the good, which is at root the thirst for God, however much this may be obscured in the course of life. Life is re-ordered by this confession, with its narrative form and its attention to desires and motivations and to the wholeness of a person's existence from start to eternity. Because it is addressed to God, and invokes the grace of Christ, it cannot be a confession of sin without at the same time being a confession of faith and a confession of praise.

This attention to the *roots of sin*, to the tension between sin and grace, and to the *re-ordering of life by attention to deep motivations*, is a constant and integral part of tradition, though often expressed in different ways. The narrative form, however much to be recommended, is not always kept, for practical interest can choose other modalities of scrutiny, such as the listing of the capital sins.[2] The capital sins did not serve quite the same function as a later listing of the ten commandments in models for the examination of conscience, since the capital sins were not viewed as deeds to be acknowledged but as tendencies of the heart found behind many actions. These were to be brought to consciousness and confessed before God if deeds themselves were to be changed and the cancer of sin removed. This effort to get at the roots of conduct appears to be much more important in early penitential tradition than a precise enumeration of misdeeds, though it exists in tension with that kind of attention to precise acts of which some persons are only capable.

For great spiritual writers, and here one might think not only of Augustine but of such persons as John Cassian and Isidore of Seville, confession of sins is ultimately a *matter between God and the sinner*. It is a constant need of daily Christian living and serves to forge and deepen a relationship with God. None of the prescriptions about canonical penance or of the admonitions to monks to confess to spiritual guides can obscure this fact. There was indeed the role that the confessor or spiritual guide could play in helping the person examine heart and conduct and in choosing appropriate penances, and thus in mediating sound confession, but this mediation was not exactly the same in canonical penance and in personal guidance. In the former it had to lead to some appropriate public acknowledgment of being a sinner and to public reconciliation with the Church.

When the *boundaries between canonical penance and other forms of confession and penance dissolved*, the confession of sin related to the sacrament in new ways, and was more constantly, and for all, related to sacramental practice, even though the possibility of confession to laypersons remained for a long time. This confession served in the first place as an intensification of the Christian life and as a means of receiving guidance from priests. It could and did also serve as a control on beliefs, made concrete in the law of confession to one's own pastor, as well as a control on ethical behaviour and universal norms of conduct in society. The more precision was asked in confession, the more these purposes were served, but the precision could also adversely affect the quality of the act of confession itself. One way of getting around this problem was to separate the act of contrition from the act of confession, but this disjunction does not really serve very well. There is a wonderful model for the celebration of penance between confessor and penitent in the work of Lanfranc of Canterbury, where he presents them as co-penitents looking to the mercy of God and united together in confession and penance in a way that reflects the unity of Jesus Christ with the Father.[3] This model acts as a counterbalance to the judicial model, but unfortunately it can all too readily be displaced by it.

In the light of this historical development of the uses of confession, it is of importance to note that it is the *failure of the role of integral confession in mediating commonly accepted ethical standards that has served most sharply to alert us today to the deficiencies and inadequacies of the sacramental practice*. In other words, today's penitential practice as prescribed by Church canons and ritual does not adequately serve the naming of sin. Quite interestingly, this failure is illustrated by an increasing appeal for *collective absolution* (repeated by a number of bishops at the Synod) and by its relative success. The quest for this form of forgiveness and reconciliation appears to be rooted in the difficulties experienced in confessing personally. These do not spring simply from an unwillingness to recognise oneself a sinner or to deal with sin in one's life. It has more to do with an uncertainty over what constitutes sin and consequently with how to name it. Collective absolution provides a port of re-entry to a shared religious identity and a shared acknowledgment of sinfulness for many who cannot take the route of individual confession in a sacramental forum. In effect, it provides a communal sign of a social nature which actually allows for a divergence of opinions on categories of sins, thus defusing the threat of a broken communal ethic. People can have resort to personal guidance and even personal confession outside the sacramental forum, while still finding a common ritual that expresses the desire for community, and forgiveness and reconciliation.

Even while seeing the benefits of a less inflated use of individual sacramental confession, and the desirability of communal rituals of reconciliation, one has to recognise the problematic affecting not only the sacrament but confession in its larger form. The diverse ministries that serve the building up of the

Church in its witness in society have to be addressed more specifically to the question of *how to discern and name sin*, and to allow people this possibility in their individual and collective lives.

The *archaic symbols of stain, deviation and guilt occur continually in the language used to express offence against moral norms*. In recent times, they were used to bring attention primarily to sexual disorders and to conduct which the Church disavowed. The shift of Catholic conscience (to speak here only of it) is marked by the ways in which these symbols are now being used of other types of action. One can note, for example, how words like 'pollution' are used to speak of social disorder or of the effects of technological progress on the environment. In the USA, to take another example, the remembrance of the war in Vietnam has become a symbol of a deviation in direction that continues to threaten the country even a decade after the end of that conflict. The sins of fatalism, individualism, greed, ambition and exploitation constitute the guilt of a new generation, rather than those of sexual behaviour.

There is a process of renaming sin going on, though for the time being it is hesitant and without clear focus. It can go with some irresponsibility regarding sexual activity, which in face of increased concern with the social and the public realm tends to get pushed into what is called the order of private morality. The answer to this, however, is not to focus anew on sexual sins, but to direct the formation of a communal conscience about social evil and at the same time to bring to light the communal and cultural implications of sexual behaviour. None of this can be brought about by a heavy emphasis on integral confession to a priest. It requires a *concentration of many ministries and activities*, some addressed to the individual, some to the community. The multiple function of the confession of sins can be retrieved by separating it, and guidance in making it, from a narrow binding to sacramental practice. There are ancient traditions and there are traditions other than the Western Catholic from which much can be learned in this regard. The formation of a communal conscience can be served by education, and in a very important way by emerging forms of communal celebrations and penance, where too the Western Catholic tradition can learn from others and from what is happening in the young churches of other continents. These celebrations do not centre around the priestly absolution, but follow the now developing eucharistic models of communal sharing and interaction in the mediation of God's grace. We hope that the articles here presented serve to bring more attention to confession itself, to current problems and directions, and to the multiple ways in which it relates to sacrament and celebration.

Notes

1. *Ordo Paenitentiae* § 6.
2. Capital sins were not always identical in number, though the number seven came to prevail.
3. *De Celanda Confessione Libellus*, PL 120, 627.

Contributors

KONRAD BAUMGARTNER was born in 1940 in Altötting, Bavaria. After studying in Passau and Munich, he became a priest in the diocese of Passau. In 1976 he became professor for pastoral theology at the University of Eichstätt, and he moved to a chair in Regensburg in 1980. Since 1969 he has edited *Der Prediger und Katechet*, a journal for homiletics, to which he also contributes. Publications: *Die Seelsorge im Bistum Passau zwischen barocker Tradition, Aufklärung und Restauration* (1975); *Erfahrungen mit dem Bußsakrament* (2 vols., 1979–80); *Das Seelsorgegespräch* in der Gemeinde (1982); *Kasualpredigten* (3 vol., 1975–83); with P. Wehrle and J. Werbick (ed.), *Glauben lernen—leben lernen. Beiträge zu Didaktik des Glaubens und der Religion* (1985); *Lebendig mitfeiern. Ansprachen zur Liturgie der Meßfeier* (1986).

DIONISIO BOROBIO was born in Spain in 1938 and ordained in Bilbao in 1965, after studies at the Gregorian University and the Liturgical Institute of St Anselmo in Rome. He is a Doctor in Liturgical Theology at the Pontifical University of Salamanca. He has written many articles and six books, including studies of 'Confirmation Today: from Theology to Practice' (1974), penitential teaching in the 'Liber Orationum Psalmographus' (1977), penance in the Spanish Church from the fourth to the seventh centuries (1978), and 'Sacraments in community' (1985).

CATHERINE DOOLEY, OP is a Dominican Sister from Sinsinawa, Wisconsin, and is currently teaching in the School of Religious Studies at Catholic University of America. She holds a doctorate in Religious Studies from the University of Louvain (KUL) and degrees from the Catholic University of America and Harvard Divinity School. She has published in *Tijdschrift voor Theologie, Questions liturgiques, The Living Light*, and *Liturgy*.

CESARE GIRAUDO, SJ was born in 1941. He gained a doctorate in theology from the Greogorian University in Rome. He has received stimulating input for his studies from his contact with the oral religious tradition of the East Coast of Madagascar. He is a lecturer in sacramental theology at the Theological Faculty (San Luigi Section) at Naples. His publications include *La sturuttura letteraria della preghiera eucaristica. Saggio sulla genesi letteraria di una forma* (tôdâ *veterotestamentaria,* b^e^rākâ *giudaica* anafora *cristiana*). Biblical Institute Press (Rome 1981). Due shortly: *Eucaristia per la Chiesa. Prospettive teologiche sull'eucaristia a partire dall'lex orandi*.

FR KABASELE-LUMBALA, aged 39, is a native of Zaire and has been a priest since 1974. He worked for four years as a curate at Cibombo in Zaire, then for five years in Paris, and for the past two years has been parish priest of Cijiba, a bush parish in the heart of Africa. He gained his doctorate of theology, specialising in liturgy, at the Institut Catholique in Paris and his doctorate in comparative religion at the Sorbonne. In addition to his parish work he is responsible for courses in catechesis and liturgy at the theological faculty of Kinshasa and is a visiting lecturer of the Lumen Vitae Institute at Brussels. He has published articles on liturgy and inculturation in journals like *Lumière et Vie* and *Bulletin de théologie africaine* and has contributed to works like *A travers le monde célébrations de l'eucharistie* (1981) and *Chemins de la christologie africaine* (1986).

NORBERT METTE is Professor of Practical Theology at the University of Paderborn. He is married and has three children. He is a member of the Editorial Committee of *Concilium*. He has published widely on questions of pastoral theology and religious education, e.g., *Voraussetzungen christlicher Elementarerziehung* (1983); *Kirche auf dem Weg ins Jahr 2000* (together with M. Blasberg-Kuhnke, 1986).

GAIL RAMSHAW-SCHMIDT is a Lutheran scholar of liturgical language. She is the author of numerous articles on the theory and use of the language of the liturgy. Her books include *Letters for God's Name* and *Christ in Sacred Speech*. She lives in New York, USA.

FRANK SENN is pastor of Christ the Mediator Lutheran Church in Chicago. He was previously professor of liturgics at the Lutheran School of Theology at Chicago. He has a PhD from the University of Notre Dame. He is author of *The Pastor as Worship Leader* (1977) and *Christian Worship and its Cultural Setting* (1983) and editor of *Protestant Spiritual Traditions* (1986) and *New Eucharistic Prayers: Development and Analysis* (1987). He was a member of the Lutheran-Episcopal Dialogue in the USA and is active in the North American Academy of Liturgy.

MICHAEL SIEVERNICH SJ was born at Arnburg, Germany, in 1945. He entered the Society of Jesus in 1965. He was ordained priest in 1973. He studied theology and philosophy in Munich, Frankfurt and Münster-Westphalia. He has made study visits to North and South America. He took his Doctorate in theology at the Westphalian Wilhelms-Universität Münster. Since 1981 he has taught pastoral theology and religious educational theory at the Philosophisch-theologische Hochschule Sankt Georgen at Frankfurt am Main. Among his publications are works on guilt and sin in modern theology, and on guilt and conversion in world religions, as well as on Friedrich Spee SJ.

FRANS VAN DE PAVERD, OSA was born in Amsterdam (the Netherlands) in 1934. Since 1954 he has been a member of the Dutch province of the Augustinian Fathers, with whom he studied philosophy and theology. From 1961 until 1964 he specialised in the theology of the Eastern Churches at the Pontificium Institutum Orientalium Studiorum in Rome. In addition to the book and the article named in the footnotes, he has also written, for example, ' "Confession" (exagoreusis) and "Penance" (exomologesis) in *De lepra* of Methodius of Olympus I–II', *OrChrP* 14 (1978), 309–341; 45 (1979), 45–74; 'Ausschluss und Wiederversöhnung in der Byzantinischen Kirche', *OstKSt* 28 (1979), 281–302 and 'Disciplinary Procedures in the Early Church', *Aug.* 21 (1981), 291–316.

GEOFFREY WAINWRIGHT was born in Yorkshire, England, in 1939. He is an ordained minister of the British Methodist Church. After studies in Cambridge, Geneva and Rome, he taught systematic theology in Yaounde (Cameroon), Birmingham (England), and Union Theological Seminary (New York). Among his works pertinent to the theme of 'confession of fault and reconciliation among the churches' are *Christian Initiation* (1969), *Eucharist and Eschatology* (1971), *Doxology* (1980), and *The Ecumenical Moment* (1983). A member of the Faith and Order Commission of the World Council of Churches, he presided over the final redaction of *Baptism, Eucharist and Ministry* at Lima in 1982. Dr Wainwright is also a member of the international dialogue between the World Methodist Council and the Roman Catholic Church. Since 1983 he has been Professor of Systematic Theology at Duke University (Durham, USA).

CONCILIUM

CONCILIUM

CONCILIUM 1986

All back issues are still in print: available from bookshops (price £4.95) or direct from the publisher (£5.45/US$8.95/Can$10.95 including postage and packing).

T & T CLARK LTD, 59 GEORGE STREET EDINBURGH EH2 2LQ, SCOTLAND

CONVERSATIONS ON COUNSELLING
Edited by Marcus Lefébure

Conversations on Counselling offers a deeply experienced and thought out spiritual interpretation of counselling work drawing on personal case-work and references to Aquinas, Augustine, Buddha, Jung and Rudolf Steiner.

"[Conversations on Counselling] is short, well written and invaluable and should be read by everybody who is concerned about human relationships and is actually doing counselling work."

Dr. Jack Dominian, Consultant Psychiatrist

Paperback £4·95

HUMAN EXPERIENCE AND THE ART OF COUNSELLING
Edited by Marcus Lefébure

A sequel to the widely read *Conversations on Counselling*, the main theme is that although counselling does involve certain professional technical skills, it remains an art which should be firmly grounded in concern, common sense, and humanity.

Paperback £4·95

T & T Clark Ltd
59 George Street, Edinburgh EH2 2LQ, Scotland